PUERTO RICO AND VIRGIN ISLANDS WILDLIFE VIEWING GUIDE

David W. Nellis

FALCON®

HELENA, MONTANA

The Governor of Puerto Rico

Greetings from America's Island of Enchantment!

Renowned for warm hospitality, exquisite beaches, Spanish-colonial archi-
tecture, state-of-the-art visitor accommodations, and vibrant nightlife,
Puerto Rico is also exceptional for its verdant mountains, lush tropical forests, exotic flowers, and fascinating variety of rare fauna.

Marvel at the humpback whales that winter in the Mona Passage off
Rincón; flocks of sea birds; the endangered hawksbill turtle; or the spectacular coral reefs of Culebra. Hike along the trails of El Yunque (the only
rain forest administered by the U.S. government) to catch a glimpse of
Amazona vittata, better known as the Puerto Rican parrot, amid more than
240 species of extraordinary flora.

The *Puerto Rico and Virgin Islands Wildlife Viewing Guide* offers a tempting
sample of what lies in store for our nature-loving guests. And when em-
barking on your journey of discovery here, by all means take the opportunity to familiarize yourself with our ecological programs on such subjects
as wildlife research, forest management, and conservation.

So bring along your binoculars, camera, diving gear, and—of course—
your spirit of adventure: The 38 Puerto Rico sites described in this book
are certain to provide you with a rich harvest of rewarding experiences.

It is a pleasure to invite you to share with us the wonders of Puerto Rico,
U.S.A.

Sincerely,

Pedro Rosselló

Pedro Rosselló

The United States Virgin Islands
Office of the Governor

The U.S. Virgin Islands, the easternmost lands flying the American flag, are an archipelago with 180 square miles of land distributed over 2,000 square miles of ocean. The islands are inhabited by many species of truly tropical wildlife and are the winter home to many of the birds, which nest on the mainland United States in the summer. The many small, uninhabited islands surrounding St. Thomas, St. John, and St. Croix are occupied by nesting colonies of otherwise seldom seen tropical sea birds. The clear, tropical waters support thriving coral reef ecosystems, which are home to many colorful fish and invertebrates. The climate is warm and sunny with the sea near 80 degrees all year, making our islands an excellent destination, year-round, for travelers who appreciate nature.

The *Puerto Rico and Virgin Islands Wildlife Viewing Guide* will help you get to sites where you can find and identify this rich mix of terrestrial, avian, and aquatic creatures, some of the most attractive and easily accessible viewing sites, and aid in your identification of some of the fascinating creatures living in the Virgin Islands while you visit the friendly island people.

A partnership of local and federal natural resource agencies and private corporations have completed this guide hoping it will give residents and visitors a better understanding of the islands' wildlife heritage and to introduce the joy of watching wildlife to those who have not had the good fortune to experience it before. We urge you to visit us in the American Caribbean.

Charles W. Turnbull
Governor of the U.S. Virgin Islands

SPONSORS

 The U.S. VIRGIN ISLANDS DEPARTMENT OF PLANNING AND NATURAL RESOURCES (DPNR), Division of Fish and Wildlife, is the primary scientific advisor on the condition of the populations of fish and wildlife, endangered and threatened species and natural habitats of the U.S. Virgin Islands. Recommendations are made on strategies that will sustain these resources for the residents of the U.S. Virgin Islands. The Division also educates residents and visitors on the importance of protecting and conserving the natural environment. For more information, contact the VI Division of Fish and Wildlife, 6291 Estate Nazareth 101, St. Thomas, VI 00802-1104; (304) 775-6762.

 The U.S. VIRGIN ISLANDS DEPARTMENT OF TOURISM is responsible for the economic development of the territory through the promotion of tourism and tourist-related activities. Other responsibilities relate to the formation, implementation, administration, and coordination of programs and policies pertaining to all aspects of tourism. For more information, contact the USVI Department of Tourism at P.O. Box 6400, St. Thomas, VI 00804; (340) 774-8784.

 DEFENDERS OF WILDLIFE is a national nonprofit organization of more than 340,000 members and supporters dedicated to preserving the natural abundance and diversity of wildlife and its habitat. A one-year membership is $20 and includes a subscription to *Defenders*, an award-winning conservation magazine. To join, or for further information, write or call Defenders of Wildlife, 1101 Fourteenth Street NW, Washington, DC 20005, (202) 682-9400.

 The USDA FOREST SERVICE is responsible for managing National Forest lands and their resources, and for protecting and restoring these lands to best serve the needs of the American people. The Caribbean National Forest is a sponsor of this program to promote awareness, enjoyment, and conservation of fish and wildlife in Puerto Rico and the U.S. Virgin Islands. Contact the Caribbean National Forest at P.O. Box 490, Palmer, PR 00721; (787) 888-1880.

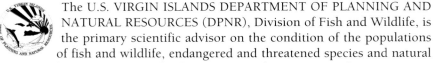 The NATIONAL OCEANIC AND ATMOSPHERIC ADMINISTRATION'S (NOAA) mission is to describe and predict changes in the Earth's environment and to conserve and manage wisely the nation's coastal and marine resources. NOAA Fisheries performs research to build sustainable fisheries, recover protected species, and sustain healthy coasts. NOAA's National Ocean Service supports and provides science, management, and leadership necessary for the environmental and economic well-being of the nation's coastal resources and communities, and oversees the National Marine Sanctuaries and National Estuarine Research Reserve System. NOAA Fisheries: www.nmfs.gov; NOAA National Ocean Service: www.nos.noaa.gov.

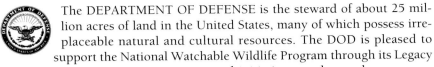

The DEPARTMENT OF DEFENSE is the steward of about 25 million acres of land in the United States, many of which possess irreplaceable natural and cultural resources. The DOD is pleased to support the National Watchable Wildlife Program through its Legacy Resource Management Program, a special initiative to enhance the conservation and restoration of natural and cultural resources on military land. For more information, contact ODUSD (ES) EQ-LP, 3400 Defense Pentagon, Room 3E791, Arlington, VA 20301-3400.

The Caribbean is a place of extraordinary natural beauty. At Coral World, we bring you close to the inhabitants of the magical undersea world that surrounds the Virgin Islands and to the stunning variety of plant life that grows in our lagoons and on our hillsides. Our goal is to entertain, to educate, and to inspire appreciation and understanding of the local environment. Our hope is that you will experience the joy of discovery, and that you will love and protect the natural treasures you see here. Contact Coral World at 6450 Coki Point, St. Thomas, VI 00802; (340) 775-1555.

The U.S. FISH AND WILDLIFE SERVICE (USFWS) is the principal federal agency responsible for conserving, protecting, and enhancing the nation's fish and wildlife and their habitats for the benefit, use, and enjoyment of the public. For further information, contact the U.S. Fish and Wildlife Service, 1875 Century Boulevard, Atlanta, GA 30345; (404) 679-4000.

© 1999 by Falcon® Publishing, Inc., Helena, Montana.
Published in cooperation with Defenders of Wildlife
Printed in Korea

1 2 3 4 5 6 7 8 9 0 CE 04 03 02 01 00 99

Project Editor: David Lee
Photo Editor: Gigette Gould
Production Editor: Larissa Berry
Copyeditor: Ginny Hoffman
Page Compositor: SRC Graphics
Book Design by Falcon Publishing, Inc.

Library of Congress Cataloging-in-Publication Data

Nellis, David W.
    Puerto Rico and Virgin Islands wildlife viewing guide / by David W. Nellis.
      p. cm.
    "Published in cooperation with Defenders of Wildlife"—T.p. verso.
    Includes index.
    ISBN 1-56044-836-9 (pbk.)
      1. Wildlife viewing sites—Puerto Rico Guidebooks. 2. Wildlife watching—Puerto Rico Guidebooks. 3. Puerto Rico Guidebooks. 4. Wildlife viewing sites—Virgin Islands of the United States Guidebooks. 5.Wildlife watching—Virgin Islands of the United States Guidebooks. 6. Virgin Islands of the United States Guidebooks. I. Defenders of Wildlife. II. Title.
    QL229.P6N45 1999
    333.95'4'097295—dc21   99-26752
                                                                                      CIP

CONTENTS

ACKNOWLEDGMENTS

There is a growing public enthusiasm for nature-based tourism in which wild animals are seen in their natural habitats. Rapid expansion in ecotourism has outpaced the traditional resources for tourist information. This book is intended to provide residents and tourists a head start on finding the "special places" for nature appreciation in Puerto Rico and the Virgin Islands. Funding was provided by the U.S. Fish and Wildlife Service, USDA Forest Service, Virgin Islands Department of Planning and Natural Resources, and Puerto Rico Department of Natural and Environmental Resources. While many individuals in the above agencies provided information in support of the preparation of this book, more extensive efforts were contributed by Brynne Bryan, Aleida Cruz, Kenneth Foote, Edgardo Gonzales, Diego Jiménez, Felix López, Robert Matos, and Frank Wadsworth. Information and assistance were also provided by John Thomlinson of the University of Puerto Rico and Alexis Molinares of the Puerto Rico Conservation Trust.

Virgin Islands Department of Planning and Natural Resources provided the services of David Nellis as the author, and the USDA Forest Service provided the services of Ricardo García as project manager.

THE NATIONAL WATCHABLE WILDLIFE PROGRAM

The National Watchable Wildlife Program is a nationwide cooperative effort to combine wildlife conservation with America's growing interest in wildlife-related outdoor recreation. The concept of the program is simple: People want to watch wildlife, and they want to watch wildlife in natural settings. But they don't always know where to go; they don't know when to go; and they don't know what to expect when they get there.

The National Watchable Wildlife Program is designed to answer those needs. Each participating state or territory identifies its best places for viewing wildlife; a uniform system of road signs (the binoculars logo you see on the cover of this guide) is put in place to help direct travelers; and guidebooks like this one give wildlife enthusiasts specific information about the sites.

The *Puerto Rico and Virgin Islands Wildlife Viewing Guide* is the 29th book in the Watchable Wildlife series that forms the cornerstone of the program. Each of the sites mentioned in this book is marked with the brown-and-white binocular logo. Similar viewing networks have been established in over half of the fifty states. Thus, the effort is part of a growing nationwide network. Though license fees and taxes paid by hunters and anglers have helped fund wildlife conservation and recreation in the past, increased conservation efforts have required additional sources of revenue. Efforts are underway at state and national levels to develop new funding mechanisms.

The Watchable Wildlife Program has been organized in Puerto Rico by the Caribbean National Forest of the U.S. Forest Service and in the U.S. Virgin Islands by the Division of Fish and Wildlife of the islands' Department of Planning and Natural Resources. As time goes on, sites will be enhanced with trails and interpretive material such as signs, bird and animal lists, and brochures.

The goal of the Watchable Wildlife Program is to make wildlife viewing fun. But in a larger context, the Watchable Wildlife Program is about conservation.

It began in 1990 with the signing of a Memorandum of Understanding by eight federal land management agencies, the International Association of Fish and Wildlife Agencies, and four national conservation groups. The program is founded on the notion that, given opportunities to enjoy and learn about wildlife in natural settings, people will become advocates for conservation in the future. The success of wildlife conservation everywhere depends on the interest and active involvement of citizens.

Use this guide to make your wildlife watching trips fun and successful; use it to discover Puerto Rico and the Virgin Islands in new ways; and as you travel around these islands, remember that these places can only exist with the support of interested citizens like you. Support conservation efforts in every way you can.

HOW TO USE THIS GUIDE

This guide is divided into seven sections, representing the principal biophysical regions of Puerto Rico and the Virgin Islands. At the beginning of each section, wildlife viewing sites are listed and located on a map. The text for each viewing site includes the following elements, which describe and interpret the habitats and the wildlife you may see. Pay attention to NOTES OF CAUTION in capital letters.

Description: Briefly explains the area, facilities, and wildlife.

Viewing Information: Expands on the site description, providing the seasonal likelihood of spotting wildlife along with other interesting information about the area. May include details about access and parking.

Directions: *Provides written directions for each site. Supplement this information with an up-to-date road map of Puerto Rico and the Virgin Islands.*

Ownership: Includes the name of the agency, organization, or company that owns or manages the site. The telephone number listed may be used to obtain more information.

Recreation and Facility Icons: Indicates some of the facilities and opportunities available at each site. The managing agency or organization can provide more information and describe other types of opportunities available.

MAP OF PUERTO RICO

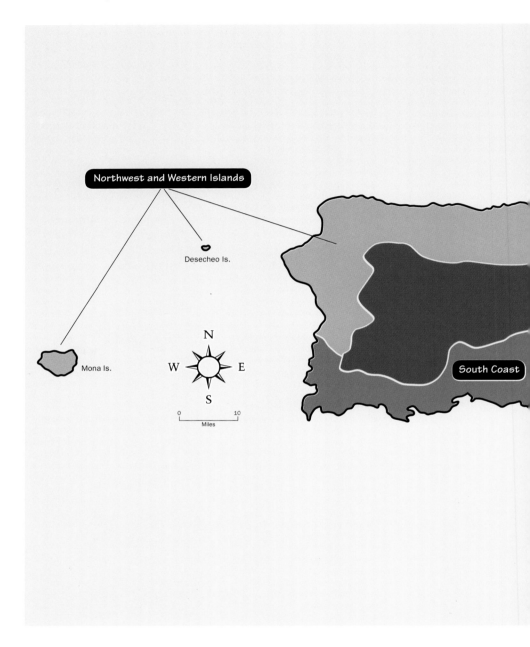

Northwest and Western Islands

Desecheo Is.

Mona Is.

South Coast

N
W   E
S

0   10
Miles

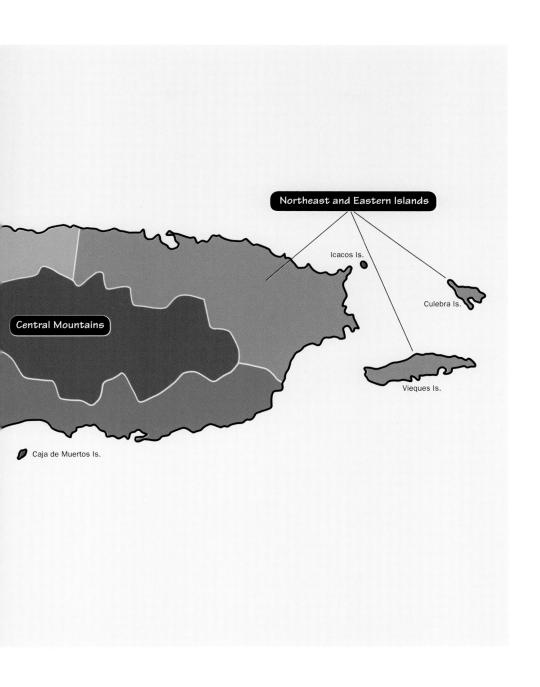

Northeast and Eastern Islands

Icacos Is.

Culebra Is.

Central Mountains

Vieques Is.

Caja de Muertos Is.

MAPS OF THE U.S. VIRGIN ISLANDS

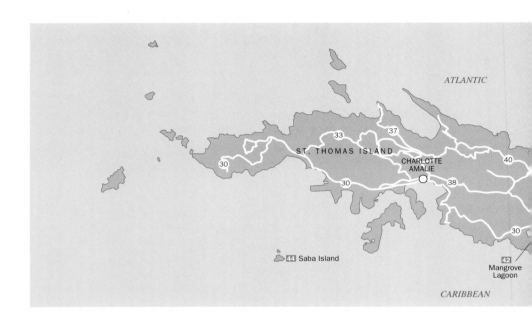

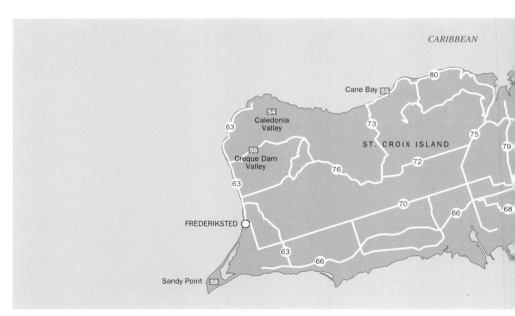

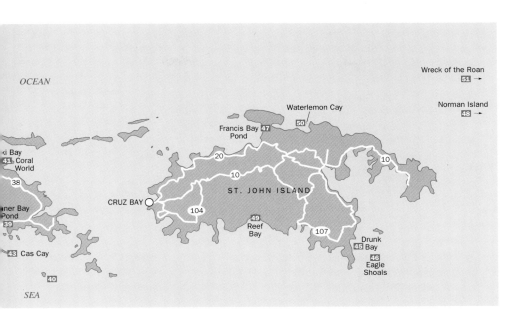

OCEAN

Wreck of the Roan
51 →

Waterlemon Cay

Norman Island
48 →

Francis Bay 47   50
Pond

i Bay
41 Coral
World

20

10

38

10

CRUZ BAY ○   ST. JOHN ISLAND

ner Bay
Pond   104

39   49
Reef
Bay   107

43 Cas Cay   Drunk
45 Bay

46
Eagle
Shoals

40

SEA

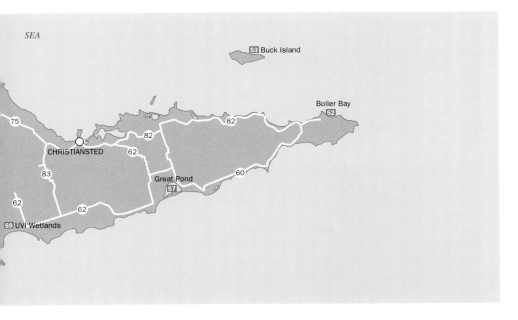

SEA

53 Buck Island

Boiler Bay

75   52

82

82   82

CHRISTIANSTED   62

83   Great Pond   60

57

62   62

59 UVI Wetlands

13

Shallow-Water Reef Fish

When snorkeling among shallow water reefs, look for these species: (1) bluestriped grunt, (2) hogfish, (3) dog snapper, (4) schoolmaster, (5) mutton snapper, (6) lane snapper, (7) rock hind, (8) red hind, (9) graysby, (10) coney, (11) redband parrotfish, (12) stoplight parrotfish, (13) jolthead porgy, (14) oldwife, and (15) black durgon.

INTRODUCTION

Geology and species evolution

In the Pleistocene era, when the seas were lower (from 100,000 to 10,000 or 12,000 years ago), Puerto Rico, St. Thomas, St. John, the British Virgin Islands, and the smaller cays and "satellite" islands off their shores formed a single, undivided landmass. Then the sea level rose and all but the uppermost mountains and highest valleys of this landmass were submerged. It is these mountains and high valleys that have become the present-day islands and have been inhabited by flora, fauna, and the human species.

St. Croix, which lies more than 30 miles south of St. Thomas and St. John, was not part of this large landmass. It lies on a separate fragment of the earth's crust. Between St. Croix and the gently sloping plateau on which the other islands rest is an oceanic trench more than two miles deep. The dive at Cane Bay described in this book (see p. 87) shows the abrupt edge of the St. Croix landmass. Divers descending there can look over the edge of the platform, where a vertical wall drops 1,500 feet toward the bottom of the trench.

This geologic gulf between St. Croix and the northern islands has played an important role in the distribution of plants and animals on the islands. Because it is removed from the other islands by an expanse of water deep and wide, St. Croix has different flora and fauna than Puerto Rico, St. Thomas, St. John, and the British Virgin Islands. As Charles Darwin showed, plants and animals that become isolated from other members of their species frequently evolve unique characteristics, eventually forming a separate species. For example, the snake known as the Puerto Rican racer, *Alsophis puertoricensis,* is abundant on Puerto Rico, St. Thomas, and St. John. A closely related species of racer was found on St. Croix, *Alsophis sancte crucis,* until the early twentieth century, when predation by mongooses rendered it extinct.

Mongooses (see p. 92) have been a profound agent of ecological change in the Virgin Islands and other places they've been introduced. They were imported on many islands, including St. Croix, at the end of the nineteenth century to control rats in sugarcane fields. *Ameiva polops,* a ground lizard once found only on St. Croix and its satellites, is now found only on some smaller cays and islands that can't be reached by mongooses. A closely related species, *Ameiva exul,* survives on St. Thomas, St. John, and Puerto Rico, despite the presence of mongooses.

Despite the array of colorful images found in this book, Puerto Rico and the Virgin Islands have fewer species of plants and animals than one would expect to find on mainland sites with a similar climate. These islands are almost equidistant from Mexico's Yucatan Peninsula and Venezuela; thus colonizing species must establish populations in a "stepping stone" fashion over other islands before reaching Puerto Rico and the Virgin Islands. Many species fail to complete the sequence. As an example, Trinidad, which is only six miles from Venezuela, has 87 species of bats. The number of bat species declines as you move north in the Lesser Antilles until you reach the Virgin Islands, which have only four species of bats.

Climate

Puerto Rico and the Virgin Islands enjoy a warm climate due to their location near the equator. The temperature is mediated by the trade winds, which blow constantly from the east. At low elevations, daily temperatures rarely drop below 70 degrees in the winter and seldom exceed 95 degrees in the summer. The climate is so uniform that the January and July average temperatures are only five degrees different. The islands experience few cloudy days. Most rainfall occurs in brief squalls from September through December.

CLIMATE/ECOLOGY

Puerto Rico has six major ecological life zones defined by their temperature, rainfall and evaporation. The driest areas are in the southwest plains of the island near Cabo Rojo and Guánica. The area of greatest rainfall is in the high eastern mountains of the Caribbean National Forest.

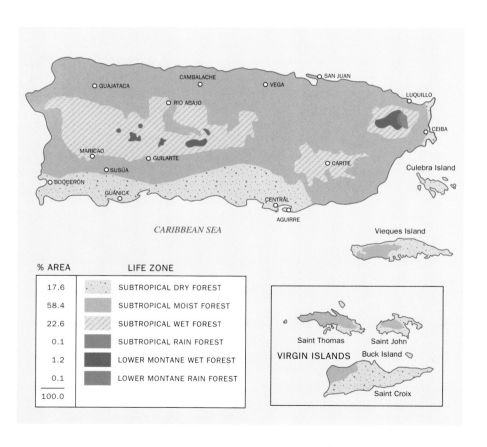

% AREA	LIFE ZONE
17.6	SUBTROPICAL DRY FOREST
58.4	SUBTROPICAL MOIST FOREST
22.6	SUBTROPICAL WET FOREST
0.1	SUBTROPICAL RAIN FOREST
1.2	LOWER MONTANE WET FOREST
0.1	LOWER MONTANE RAIN FOREST
100.0	

WILDLIFE VIEWING AND STEWARDSHIP PRINCIPLES

Observing wildlife in their natural habitat is one of life's great pleasures. When you watch wildlife without causing a disruption, you are witnessing the truly wild. Learn the basics, follow the principles explained below, and, with all due respect, immerse yourself into the world of nature.

Look in the right place, at the right time

Both of these are crucial for successful wildlife viewing. Many species live only in specific habitats, such as rain forests, mangroves, or coral reefs. Some may be unique or endemic to specific islands. In addition, the time of day or season is an important factor to consider in looking for wildlife. Some species such as mongooses, gulls, and terns are only active during the day, while others such as the St. Thomas tree boa, the cave bat, and the Jamaican fruit bat are only active at night. Seasonal migrations are also important for many species of birds and marine mammals such as humpback whales, which come to the warm waters of the Caribbean during the winter to breed and nurse their young.

Keep your distance

Wild animals are sensitive to human disturbance. Resist the temptation to move close to them. Use binoculars, spotting scopes, and zoom lenses to get a closer view. If an animal changes its behavior—if it stops feeding, raises its head sharply, appears nervous or aggressive, changes its direction of travel, exhibits a broken wing display, or circles repeatedly—move away slowly. If a wild animal approaches you, stay calm, and try to back away. Maintain your distance from nests, rookeries, and resting areas.

Do not touch any animal, even if it appears to be sick, injured, or orphaned

Animals that appear to be sick or injured may actually be resting. Young animals that seem orphaned may have parents that are either foraging or observing nearby. Closely approaching these animals may interfere with parental care. If you see an animal that you believe is injured or orphaned, call the local wildlife authorities for assistance and advice.

Do not use calls, whistles, or other artificial means to attract wildlife

Calls, whistles, and recordings may disturb and confuse wildlife and interfere with their communication.

Never feed wild animals

Feeding wildlife is known to be harmful and can keep young animals from learning important survival skills. Animals can become sick or die from ingesting unnatural or contaminated food items. Feeding them can also habituate animals to humans, which is dangerous to both species.
Please remember that feeding some species, such as marine mammals, is against the law.

Coral Reef Fish

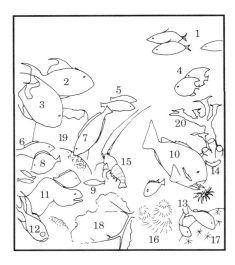

Swimming among the coral reefs are (1) bar Jack, (2) queen triggerfish, (3) French angelfish, (4) queen angelfish, (5) red hind, (6) schoolmaster, (7) redtail parrotfish, (8) blue tang, (9) fairy basslet, (10) Nassau grouper, (11) green moray, (12) squirrelfish, (13) French grunt, and (14) neon goby. The reef life also includes (15) spiny lobster, (16) Christmas tree worm, (17) star coral, (18) sea fan, (19) basket sponge, and (20) elkhorn coral.

Leave pets at home

Wild and domesticated animals do not mix. Pets may startle, chase, and even kill wildlife. Likewise, pets can be injured or killed by a threatened or disturbed wild animal.

Respect the rights of other wildlife viewers

Move slowly and quietly and keep on designated trails to protect habitat and avoid trampling vegetation, disturbing wildlife, and contributing to erosion.

Respect the rights of landowners

Get permission before entering private property.

Take only memories and leave only footprints

Please pick up and dispose of trash properly.

Share the joy of wildlife viewing with others, especially children, and teach them about the importance of not disturbing wild animals or habitat.

SPECIAL CONSIDERATIONS FOR MARINE WILDLIFE

The Caribbean islands offer a unique opportunity to view terrestrial, coastal, and marine wildlife within the following habitats: tropical rain forests, subtropical dry forests, grasslands, fringing mangroves, mud flats, beaches, rocky shores, sea grass beds, coral reefs, and open ocean waters. Numerous species of marine life can be seen from the shore and in coastal environments. Brown pelicans, red-cheeked pintails, royal terns, brown boobies, hawksbill sea turtles, West Indian manatees, spotted and bottlenose dolphins, humpback whales, and a variety of marine fish and invertebrates make up vibrant Caribbean coral reef and sea grass communities.

Marine biologists have observed many incidences of marine life harmed or disturbed by people, often unintentionally: sea bird chicks abandoned by their parents after frequent close approaches; coral reefs damaged from grounded boats, dropped anchors, or breakage by inexperienced swimmers and divers; dolphins and manatees hit by inattentive boaters; colonies of beach-nesting shore birds or turtles harassed by uncontrolled pets; and animals injured or sickened by ingesting human food, fishing hooks, nets, garbage, and other human debris.

Keep in mind that marine animals are wild and should be given the same consideration as terrestrial wildlife. Follow the principles listed above when you are in the marine environment. In particular, please be careful not to:
• chase, handle, or feed marine animals.
• discard fishing line, nets, plastics, or garbage in the water.
• discharge sewage or other pollutants in or near the water.

When in the vicinity of coral reefs and sea grass beds, please remember the following coral reef and sea grass bed etiquette:
• corals are living animals and are very fragile. Touching them may cause damage. Be careful so that your hands, knees, fins, gauges, or tank do not touch the coral.

Mangrove Habitat

Birds of the mangrove include (1) white-crowned pigeon, (2) yellow warbler, (3) yellow-crowned night heron, (4) Antillean mango hummingbird, and (5) white-cheeked pintail. A green iguana (6) rests atop the mangrove roots. In the waters of the mangrove are (7) juvenile parrotfish, (8) four-eyed butterfly fish, (9) great barracuda, (10) red-backed cleaning shrimp, (11) juvenile French grunt, and (12) the mangrove crab.

- do not collect corals, shells, sand dollars, or sea stars.
- respect environmental laws and game limits.
- use mooring buoys whenever available or carefully anchor in sand. Do not allow the anchor or chain to come in contact with coral or sea grass beds.
- when in a boat, avoid areas which appear brown in color. Shallow reef areas and sea grass beds will appear brown. If you run aground, immediately turn the engine off. Do not try to motor off—your propeller can cause even more serious damage. Wait until high tide to remove the vessel.
- Be aware of scuba divers—watch for their dive flags and do not motor near them.

MANGROVES
by Ariel Lugo

Mangrove is a generic term used to describe tropical trees that are capable of living in seawater with their roots in a salty soil devoid of oxygen. Several plant families and numerous genera have individual species which may grow as mangroves. In Florida and the Caribbean, we regularly find three species of mangroves, named for their predominant bark color, and an associated tree called buttonwood, named for the resemblance of its fruit to old-fashioned shoe buttons.

Red mangroves grow in the water of shallow, protected areas with soft soil. They send out aerial, stilt-like roots, which stabilize the plant and allow it to grow in water as deep as three feet. The conspicuous, tapered cylindrical embryo plants of red mangroves float vertically and are dispersed by water currents until their lower end lodges in mud. They then take root and start a new tree. The roots are able to take in water while excluding salt, and the bark has small openings called lenticels, which allow gas exchange. Red mangroves are favorite nesting areas for white-crowned pigeons, and frequently provide roosting sites for pelicans and herons, where they are safe from land-based predators.

Black mangroves grow on the landward side of red mangroves and can tolerate salt better than any other Caribbean mangrove. They maintain salt balance by excreting salt from the surface of their leaves. Black mangroves can grow in water three times as salty as seawater.

White mangroves generally grow inland from red mangroves in areas not routinely inundated by tides. They may develop short "prop" roots from the lower trunk for stability and respiratory roots which extend above the soil for gas exchange.

Buttonwood is tolerant of salt in the soil, but does not thrive in wet soils lacking oxygen.

Red mangroves resist wave action by extending prop roots into shallow water. The roots become encrusted by many invertebrates and provide refuge and food for juvenile reef fish.
DAVID W. NELLIS

MIGRATION: ENRICHMENT OF THE CARIBBEAN AVIFAUNA
by Joseph M. Wunderle, Jr.

As they move between their northern breeding grounds and southern wintering grounds, hundreds of thousands of migrant birds pass through Puerto Rico and the Virgin Islands, most of them unnoticed. It's a spectacular feat. Consider the blackpoll warbler: This bird usually weighs 16 grams, but doubles its weight in New England before flying for 85 hours over the Atlantic and Caribbean to its wintering grounds in Venezuela. A few blackpolls visit our islands briefly each October, but for most, the migration is a nonstop flight.

To navigate this awesome journey, the birds take a combination of cues from the sun, the stars, and magnetic fields, as demonstrated by other migrants. Apparently, their navigational abilities are outstanding. Banding studies on other birds in Puerto Rico demonstrate that many migrants return to their exact wintering site year after year.

Migrants play an important role in Caribbean bird life. Approximately 50 to 60 percent of the species found here are nonbreeding migrants. Southbound migrants appear as early as July, when sandpipers from the Arctic begin to appear here on *salinas* (salt marshes or ponds) and beaches. Most of the migrants head to South America by November, but some linger until April and then head north. Some sandpipers and plovers also stop on their way north in the spring, but most northbound shorebirds bypass the islands.

Migrant warblers begin appearing in August and many overwinter here in various habitats where some establish small territories that they defend from others of their kind. Curiously, some male warbler migrants, such as American redstarts and black-throated blue warblers, compete with females of their species, occupying some forest areas and relegating the females to shrubby second-growth habitats. Other warblers join mixed species flocks in some forests. Even some territorial species abandon their territories at sunset to roost with other warblers, particularly in the drier habitats.

Scientists have found that migration evolves in birds wherever the conditions and resources are suitable during the breeding season but inadequate at other times of year. Thus, about 10 species breed in Puerto Rico and the Virgin Islands, then migrate elsewhere when not breeding. The black-whiskered vireo, for instance, is found in abundance breeding in the forests of our islands, but departs for South America in September and stays there until January. In contrast, the same bird is a year-round resident of Hispaniola and the Lesser Antilles.

The exceptional mobility of birds allows them to take advantage of the seasonal fluctuations of resources by moving between sites that may be thousands of miles apart, thus demonstrating the wonder of migration.

DRIVING IN PUERTO RICO AND THE VIRGIN ISLANDS

The highway system in Puerto Rico uses a mixed system of measurements. The speed limit is listed as miles per hour but the distances on information signs are in kilometers. The speedometers and odometers in rental cars are usually in miles. Many of the older roads had white, kilometer-marking (km) posts showing every tenth of a kilometer starting from a large town. Many of these signs are now missing, but if you see one it will help you get oriented. For instance, if you are looking for the Humacao Refuge at km 74.3 and you see a marker for 72.3, you will know your destination is only 2 kilometers farther even if many of the intervening markers are absent. Remember, a mile equals 1.6 kilometers.

The signs identifying intersections may be missing in one direction but present in the opposite direction. Thus, if you think you are near a desired intersection, it is good to slow and read the signs on the opposite side of the road after you pass through the intersection.

In the Virgin Islands, traffic drives on the left but all the vehicles are designed to drive on the right side of the road. Thus, the driver rides next to the ditch and cannot see to pass until he has pulled into the opposite lane of traffic. Passing is hazardous and not recommended on the hilly, curvy roads.

NORTHWEST PUERTO RICO AND WESTERN ISLANDS

The brown booby eats fish which it catches by plunging into the sea at high speed.
JOSÉ COLÓN

1. MONA ISLAND RESERVE

Description: Halfway between Puerto Rico and the Dominican Republic, Mona is the most remote of the Puerto Rican islands. Because of its remoteness and beauty, it is often referred to as the Galapagos of the Caribbean. Accessible by boat, Mona is a large block of eroded limestone with many deep cracks and caves. Most of the island is rimmed with steep cliffs. The bedrock is often visible under the canopy of the tropical dry forest. Typical vegetation on the surface of the island is thorny brush.

Viewing Information: Sea birds nest on Mona almost every month of the year. Brown and red-footed boobies as well as red-billed and white-tailed tropicbirds nest in the fall and winter. In the spring and summer, sooty terns nest in a large colony on grassy ledges on the northwest cliffs, while noddy terns nest in niches in the cliff face and bridled terns seek nest sites under rocks, sedges, or woody shrubs. The green iguana runs up trees, while the much sturdier ground iguana seldom climbs, seeking refuge in the abundant deep caves and cracks. Pigs, goats, chickens, cats, and rats have all been introduced and live among the scrubby, thorny vegetation. The surrounding reefs offer excellent diving with clear water, magnificent scenery, and lots of large fish such as groupers, snappers, and moray eels. Turtles, sharks, whales, and dolphins are more common here than most places in the Caribbean.

Directions: *Most trips to the island are by private boats, charter boats, and organized tours. Scheduled boats leave from Mayagüez and Cabo Rojo. The trip is 4 to 6 hours long and sometimes rough, but you will be rewarded with unique viewing opportunities on land and under water. A permit from the Department of Natural and Environmental Resources is required for overnight camping.*

Ownership: Puerto Rico Department of Natural and Environmental Resources, P.O. Box 9066600, Puerta de Tierra, San Juan, PR 00906; (787) 724-2816

Size: 14,000 acres　　**Closest Town:** Mayagüez is 40 miles to the east.

Bridled terns feed far offshore on squid, flying fish, and other small creatures typically found in association with floating sargasso weed.

DAVID W. NELLIS

25

Description: Desecheo is a steep, rocky island covered with a tropical dry forest. Large gumbo-limbo trees are common in interior valleys while a variety of cactus species, including the endangered higo chumbo, form a part of the thorny scrub vegetation covering the steep coastal slopes. At one time, many pelagic sea birds nested on the island, but the introduction of goats and monkeys has resulted in disturbance and severe habitat degradation. Due to the presence of unexploded military ordnance, visitors are prohibited from landing on the island. Anchoring while diving or bird watching is unregulated.

Viewing Information: Brown boobies, bridled terns, red-footed boobies, oystercatchers, and red-billed and white-tailed tropicbirds can be seen along the shoreline, and brown noddies nest on the cliffs. Rhesus monkeys were introduced to the island many years ago and are now proving resistant to removal. Scenic reefs surround the island. On the trip to and from the island you may see three species of dolphins. In the winter you may hear the eerie singing of humpback whales when they dive. The water is very clear and the bottom topography offers walls, canyons, and patch reefs inhabited by many species of reef fish including queen triggerfish and black durgon.

Directions: *The island is 12 miles west of the town of Rincón which can be reached by traveling north on Highway 2 from Mayagüez to the junction of Hwy 115. Follow Hwy 115 west eight miles to the village of Rincón. Commercial dive boat operators in Rincón and other west coast cities take regularly scheduled trips to Desecheo Island.*

Ownership: U.S. Fish and Wildlife Service, P.O. Box 510, Boquerón, PR 00622; (787) 851-7258

Size: 380 acres   **Closest Town:** Rincón

The brown noddy is in our area for the spring and summer while it nests on ledges on cliff faces.
JOSÉ COLÓN

EXOTICS: THE ISLAND INVADERS

by Joseph M. Wunderle, Jr.

Humans have been introducing animals to Caribbean islands since the arrival of the Amerindians. The indigenous people are believed to have introduced a variety of animals including dogs, pigs, agoutis, tortoises, guinea pigs, and possibly hutias to various islands. The invasion of exotics continued with the arrival of the Europeans who introduced various domesticated animals. However, the inadvertent introduction of rats, and the deliberate introduction of mongooses to kill rats in the sugar cane fields, were by far the most destructive introductions to the native fauna. Exotic animals have played a major role in the extinctions of Caribbean animals as a result of predation and competition, and possibly as sources of exotic diseases.

Birds have been among these introductions which have increased in the recent past as islanders have had more discretionary income. In Puerto Rico, most exotic birds escaped from the pet trade. The abundance of exotic birds in Puerto Rico is the highest for the region, with 31 species established as permanent and presumed breeders. These exotics are represented by diverse New World parrots and parakeets and a variety of finches, some from the New World and others from Africa, Asia, and Indonesia.

Whereas the pet trade brought most of the exotic birds to these islands, the subtropical climate and appropriate habitats enabled escapees to become established in the wild. The exotics have benefited from the substantial alteration of natural habitats by the Europeans, which has increased the forest edge habitats, scrubby second growth, and grasslands favored by these species. The exotic birds have yet to invade the mature, relatively undisturbed forests of Puerto Rico and are still largely confined to sites near human habitation. Some are most abundant in urban or suburban areas where they feed on fruits or seeds of exotic plants. There is no evidence as yet that the exotic birds have had a detrimental effect on the native birds, but legitimate concern exists and efforts are underway to halt the introduction of new species.

Red-footed tortoises have been widely introduced in the Caribbean. They are very hardy and able to reproduce in the wild under a broad variety of conditions.
DAVID W. NELLIS

3. CRASHBOAT BEACH

Description: This underwater site in Aguadilla Bay is actually the pilings from an old pier constructed as a base for crashboats, which rescued pilots who ditched while coming and going from the nearby Ramey Air Base. Fuel supply ships moored to the four clusters of pilings in 35 feet of water while unloading via the pipeline that can still be seen on the pier. A breakwater and slips near shore provided protection for the rescue boats. The shoreline is a broad, sandy beach which draws crowds on weekends and holidays.

Viewing Information: Grunts, parrotfish, sergeant majors, surgeon fish, many types of anemones, and colorful sponges are always visible while snorkeling or scuba diving from shore. Young French angels, black bar soldier fish, and jack-knife fish swim in the shade under the concrete slabs of the old pier. Many of these fish, as well as flounder and stingrays, can be seen by snorkeling among the slips. The full variety of fish and invertebrates is most evident at night, when lobster, octopus, and scorpionfish are more active. The polyps of the many types of corals open at night, giving a very different view of the reef than that seen in the daytime. Brown boobies and brown pelicans are present all year and feed alongside laughing gulls and several species of terns in the spring and summer. A flock of grackles lives in the mangroves of a tidal creek and scrounges scraps at the picnic tables.

Directions: From Mayagüez or Arecibo take Highway 2 to Aguadilla. Turn west on Hwy 107 and follow it two miles as it curves north. At the Crashboat Beach sign, turn left on Hwy 458 for one mile to the public parking area.

Ownership: Government of Puerto Rico

Size: 5 acres   **Closest Town:** Aguadilla

The highly camou-flaged scorpionfish lurks among rocks and coral waiting for prey to swim near. They are called scorpionfish because of venomous dorsal spines which produce painful punctures when the fish is stepped on in shallow water.
STEVE SIMONSEN

4. GUAJATACA CLIFFS

Description: A vista point for the Guajataca Cliffs is accessible from the westbound lane of Highway 2 west of Quebradillas. The old railroad bed through the tunnel and along the cliffs has been smoothed into a pleasant walkway.

Viewing Information: The overlook often has white-tailed tropicbirds soaring above it. The birds nest in small cavities in the cliffs in the winter and spring and swoop above the breaking surf to the north. The rocks have many blowholes in which wave action causes spouting of water and spray, reminiscent of a whale blowing. Cave swallows nest in recesses inside the old Guajataca railroad tunnel, 0.5 mile beyond the lookout, and on cliffs above the pathway. If you turn your back to the sea about 100 yards beyond the tunnel, you can see where about 50 pairs of these swallows build their nests below the overhanging cliffs. Wind-pruned shrubs, including ficus and sea grape, cling to the east side of the cliff through which the tunnel was bored.

Directions: *From San Juan, take Highway 22 west until it ends just past Arecibo. Continue west on Hwy 2 until just past Quebradillas, where you can stop at an overlook of the cliffs and find many sea birds soaring. The unmarked tunnel exit is to the right 0.5 mile farther down the road, at the far end of the bridge over the Guajataca River. Turn left at the T-intersection and park near the beach. Access to the tunnel, trail, and beach beyond is via the old roadbed, which passes several bars that share a taste for very loud music.*

Ownership: Private and Government of Puerto Rico

Size: 10 acres   **Closest Town:** The town of Aguadilla is 28 miles to the west, beyond the village of Quebradillas.

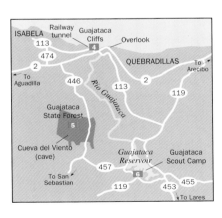

The cave swallow nests in caves and under cliff overhangs and bridges from whence it ventures forth to catch flying insects over forest, field, and open water.
JOSÉ COLÓN

5. GUAJATACA STATE FOREST

Description: This state forest is made up of a tropical karst topography, in which porous limestone rock is dissolved by rainfall and groundwater, leaving a unique, jagged landscape composed of haystack hills (*mogotes*) and many caves. The caves in the rock range in size from small slots suitable for sheltering snakes to gaping mouths large enough to admit an adult human. The sinuous paved road through the closed canopy of the humid, subtropical forest is often not wide enough for two vehicles to pass safely but affords a great view of the forest. A roadside picnic area occupies the mouth of a partially obstructed cave.

Viewing Information: The exuberant vegetation of this forest includes 186 species of trees, 23 of which are found only in Puerto Rico. The grass-like terrestrial bromeliad *Pitcairnia* drapes its slender leaves and stalks of scarlet flowers over many of the road banks. The Puerto Rican boa is common in the area and may be seen along the trails while it is hunting birds and rodents, or lurking near the mouths of caves, waiting for the evening flight of bats. This is a good place to see the lizard cuckoo, ruddy quail-dove, and red-legged thrush. Puerto Rican birds endemic to the forest include the Puerto Rican woodpecker, Puerto Rican tody, bullfinch, Puerto Rican screech owl, Puerto Rican vireo, and the tiny emerald hummingbird.

Directions: *From San Juan, take Highway 22 west about 50 miles; then continue west on Hwy 2 for 15 miles to Hwy 446. Turn left and drive south 5 miles on Hwy 446 to the forest.*

Ownership: Puerto Rico Department of Natural and Environmental Resources, P.O. Box 9066600, Puerta de Tierra, San Juan, PR 00906; (787) 724-2816

Size: 2,357 Acres

Closest Towns: Arecibo to the northeast and Mayagüez to the southwest are cosmopolitan cities. Nearby to the south is the small mountain town of San Sebastián.

The red-legged thrush is common in many forested areas of Puerto Rico where it eats fruits and insects.
BRUCE HALLETT

6. GUAJATACA SCOUT CAMP

Description: In an area of steeply rolling hills, the Boy Scout Camp occupies a forested tract on Guajataca Lake. This site was a sugar cane field which has now been reforested with a mixture of non-native and native trees, providing a habitat with lots of ecological diversity.

Viewing Information: In the winter, ospreys often feed on large bass while kingfishers dive for smaller fish near shore. Year-round, common moorhens, gallinules, and herons stalk the shoreline while grebes dive beneath the surface farther from shore. On land, todies, anis, quail-doves, and scaly-naped and white-crowned pigeons can be seen regularly. This is a particularly good site to spot owls at dusk or hear them after dark.

Directions: From San Juan, take Highway 22 west past Arecibo and turn south on Hwy 119. Turn east one mile on Hwy 455. The Boy Scout Camp is marked with a sign set back from the road on the right.

Ownership: Puerto Rico Council, Boy Scouts of America, Sacarello 1016, Urb. San Martin, Rio Pedras, PR 00924; (787) 767-0320

Size: 170 acres

Closest Towns: The small town of San Sebastián is 8 miles to the southwest. The cosmopolitan city of Arecibo is 12 miles to the northeast.

The commonly seen great blue heron is the largest of the herons in this area but is quite wary of approach. Feeding is often by standing and waiting until prey venture close enough to be captured with a stab of the beak. They eat fish, crabs, reptiles, and may forage on land for grasshoppers.
PETE CARMICHAEL

31

7. CAMBALACHE STATE FOREST

Description: This is one of the few preserved areas of lowland forest growing on the limestone of a karst landscape. The trails and overgrown access roads winding through the haystack-shaped hills, known as *mogotes*, provide easy hiking, often under a shady canopy. This forest is noted for its nursery which gives away seedling trees to help landowners reforest.

Viewing Information: This site supports most of the lowland forest birds found in Puerto Rico. White-crowned and scaly-naped pigeons feed on fruit in the canopy while zenaida doves and ground doves search for seeds on the roads and open areas. Three species of quail-doves—ruddy, Key West, and bridled—feed on seeds and invertebrates in the deep shade of the closed-canopy forest. Swallows nest in the entrances of some of the many caves. Endemic birds include the Puerto Rican tody and Puerto Rican woodpecker. Neotropical migrants live in the forest in the winter. The Puerto Rican boa is moderately abundant and is most likely encountered at dawn and dusk. After dark, the sky is occupied by many species of bats. The commonest is the Jamaican fruit bat. Also present are the rare red fig-eating bat and the endemic Caribbean cave bat.

Directions: *From San Juan take Highway 22 (the toll expressway) west toward Arecibo for 38 miles and exit on Hwy 140 north to Barceloneta. After about 1 mile turn west on Hwy 682 for 2.2 miles to the entrance sign on the north side of the road.*

Ownership: Puerto Rico Department of Natural and Environmental Resources, P.O. Box 9066600, Puerta de Tierra, San Juan, PR 00906; (787) 724-2816

Size: 2,213 acres   **Closest Town:** All tourist facilities are available 10 miles west in Arecibo.

The Jamaican fruit bat roosts in groups in caves or even in trees with thick canopies. They fly at dusk to seek ripe juicy fruit.

TOMÁS A. CARLO

8. TORTUGUERO LAGOON NATURE RESERVE

Description: Tortuguero Lagoon is the only significant natural freshwater lake in Puerto Rico. It is kept filled to above sea level by local surface runoff and springs which originate in the nearby karst hills. Highway 686 along the north side of the lagoon is built on the landward side of a sand dune covered with sea grape and coconut trees. The ocean side of the dunes provides miles of beach.

Viewing Information: The large areas of open water are used by white-cheeked pintails along with least and pied-billed grebes year-round. Many migrants join them in the winter, including ruddy ducks. Caribbean coots, purple gallinules, and sora rails feed in the shoreline vegetation. The alligator-like South American caiman has been introduced and is thriving in the lagoon. Fishermen catch tarpon, snook, and jacks in the overflow canal and large-mouth bass, sunfish, and tilapia in the main lagoon. The moist, acid soil along the shoreline supports a broad diversity of wetland plants including seven species of insectivorous plants. In the adjacent upland, the black-cowled oriole is revealed by its early morning repertoire of whistled calls and flocks of anis by their querulous *"whaat"* calls. Throughout the day, flocks of noisy Antillean grackles move along the shoreline. The bananaquit is ubiquitous and the Puerto Rican woodpecker announces its presence by drumming.

Directions: *From San Juan, take Hwy 22 west 50 miles and exit to Hwy 2 west of Vega Baja. Turn north on Hwy 687, 0.8 mile to the sign marking the dirt access road to the boat ramp, bathrooms, picnic shelters, and fishing deck.*

Ownership: Puerto Rico Department of Natural and Environmental Resources, P.O. Box 9066600, Puerta de Tierra, San Juan, PR 00906; (787) 724-2816

Size: 2,580 acres   **Closest Towns:** Vega Baja, Manatí

The purple gallinule is able to walk across lilypads while foraging, dispersing its weight with its long toes. They feed on seeds, snails, and insects.
PETE CARMICHAEL

33

NORTHEAST PUERTO RICO AND EASTERN ISLANDS

The natural beauty of Puerto Rico is readily evident even within the hustle and bustle of the capital city, San Juan. This is a region of great diversity, from urban parks to mangrove forests, marshes, rushing mountain streams, and cloud forest. Culebra and Vieques Islands and their associated cays offer white sand beaches, coral reefs, and nesting seabirds and turtles. A world-class display of the fascinating phenomenon of bioluminescence can be readily observed both at Cabezas de San Juan and at Bahía Puerto Mosquito in Vieques. The Caribbean National Forest is probably the most easily accessible tropical rainforest in the world, where lizards, coquís (Puerto Rico's tiny singing frogs), and birds like the lizard cuckoo, scaly-naped pigeon, and Puerto Rican tanager abound.

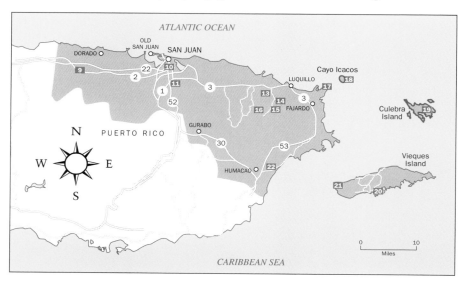

9. VEGA ALTA STATE FOREST

Description: The forest is in an area of karst topography, where rainfall and groundwater dissolve limestone. The steep hillsides are covered with native tree species and the valley bottoms have been planted with teak and pine.

Viewing Information: A nature trail winds around a hill and up the bottom of a valley with only a slight grade. The closed tree canopy 80 feet above the trail drops fruit and flowers on the forest floor. Cave swallows swoop on insects above the canopy while Puerto Rican flycatchers sing their distinctive *"whee-a-wit-whee"* song and snap up their prey in the open areas of the forest. The Puerto Rican brown racer is commonly seen gliding off the trail to disappear in the undergrowth, while at dawn and dusk coquis of several species overwhelm the forest with their calls. If you sit still, you may see or hear the slight rustling produced by the dwarf gecko, which dwells in the leaf litter. The larger and more aggressive Ameiva lizards patrol open areas while the smaller Anoles rest on the trees.

Directions: *From San Juan, take Highway 22 west 18 miles past the second toll booth and exit to Hwy 2. Turn left and travel 0.25 mile to the first traffic light. Turn right onto Hwy 690 for 150 yards, then left at the т-intersection with Hwy 676. The forest headquarters will be on your left 0.8 mile after you leave Hwy 2. The sign Bosque de Vega is 50 feet back in the trees on the other side of a 6-foot chainlink fence which borders the road. If you pass a cemetery on your left, you've just missed the entrance.*

Ownership: Puerto Rico Department of Natural and Environmental Resources, P.O. Box 9066600, Puerta de Tierra, San Juan, PR 00906; (787) 724-2816

Size: 1,245 acres of land composed of six unconnected pieces.

Closest Town: The forest headquarters is on the edge of the small town of Vega Alta.

The bananaquit is one of the most common upland birds in the Caribbean and regularly feeds on nectar and at feeders supplied with granular sugar. The nest is a closely knit hollow ball of grass and plant fibers.
PETE CARMICHAEL

Description: An elevated concrete walkway runs along the canal from San Juan Bay past Parque Central to the Mercantile Plaza in Hato Rey. It may be entered from either end and is wheelchair accessible. The walkway divides the open waters of the canal from a forest of red, black, and white mangroves which arch over the walkway. Many interpretive signs about the adjacent ecological communities are placed along the path.

Viewing Information: Many birds are present in Parque Central before you enter the boardwalk. Ground doves, zenaida doves, greater Antillean grackles, and exotic Java sparrows feed on the lawns and several species of hummingbirds sip nectar from flowering trees. On the mangrove side of the walkway, several species of tree-climbing crabs are hunted by night herons. The great egret and snowy egret are usually present in small numbers. On the canal side of the walk, snook and tarpon up to 200 pounds can be seen rolling at the surface while mullet make spectacular leaps from the water.

Directions: *From San Juan's Condado area of resort hotels, travel west on Ashford Avenue to Luís Muñoz Rivera Avenue (Highway 1) and follow it about 2.5 miles southeast to the exit signs for Parque Central. In the park, follow the main road to a parking area. A mural marks the entrance to the walkway.*

Ownership: City of San Juan

Size: The walkway is 1.2 miles long.

Closest Town: This serene park is in the middle of urban San Juan.

When hooked, tarpon jump and tail walk as they provide great excitement, but they often manage to throw the hook and escape before being landed.

STEVE SIMONSEN

36

Description: The botanical garden is a serene island of green and quiet amidst the hustle and bustle of San Juan. The well-maintained park allows quiet contemplation, a brisk walk in delightful surroundings, or serious botanical study of the more than 200 species of cultivated plants. Special sections of the garden are devoted to the growing of heliconias, bamboos, orchids, and aquatic plants as well as tropical trees from all parts of the world.

Viewing Information: San Juan has many introduced exotic bird species which like to use the grounds of the botanical garden. Some of the most common are various finches and canary-winged parakeets along with other parrots and parakeets. Domestic ducks and geese in the ponds are sometimes joined by their wild brethren. Native birds nesting in the summer but present all year include the Puerto Rican screech owl, pearly-eyed thrasher, Puerto Rican woodpecker, hummingbirds, smooth-billed ani, kestrel, and green heron.

Directions: *From Santurce, Condado, or Hato Rey travel south on Highway 1 (Luis Muñoz Rivera) to the exit to Hwy 3. Exit to the left, then keep to the left through an underpass. Follow the left lane to the first left turn lane with a traffic light. Cross with the light and the entrance sign Jardin Botanico Sur will be directly ahead.*

Ownership: University of Puerto Rico

Size: The developed part of the botanical garden is about 50 acres.

Closest Town: The botanical garden is in the Rio Piedras area of metropolitan San Juan.

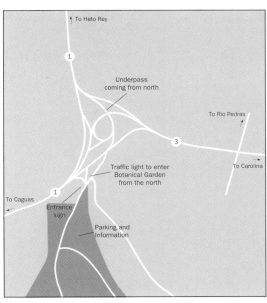

NORTHEAST PUERTO RICO AND EASTERN ISLANDS

37

12. PIÑONES STATE FOREST

Description: This state forest, the nearest to San Juan, is one of the largest mangrove forests left in the Caribbean. Highway 187 parallels miles of beach, occasionally separated from it by a dune anchored in place by coconut palms, sea grape, and casuarina trees. South of the highway is the main mangrove forest interspersed with creeks and lagoons.

Viewing Information: The open water areas are best seen from a kayak or canoe. Pelicans, ospreys, and terns dive for small fish while frigate birds soar overhead. Cave swallows and Caribbean martins catch insects above the water and mangroves. Caribbean coots, common moorhens, great blue herons, green herons, and egrets feed in the shallow waters. White-crowned pigeons roost in red mangroves year-round and nest in the spring and summer. The nature trail is muddy and its low spots are often covered by several inches of water. Herds of hermit crabs scamper off the trail waving their large left claws and attracting night herons early in the morning and at dusk. The crab's left claw is waved as a courtship display but is also used to collect food. Yellow warblers and northern waterthrush are common in the mangroves.

Directions: From the intersection with Highway 26, take Hwy 187 (also called Avenue Los Gobernadores or Avenue Boca de Cangrejos) east across a large bridge, then 1.8 miles to a sign marking the Department of Natural and Environmental Resources recreation area. Turn right and travel about 1.2 miles to the headquarters. At the headquarters, walk past three houses and continue across a fallow field to the nature trail.

Ownership: Puerto Rico Department of Natural and Environmental Resources, P.O. Box 9066600, Puerta de Tierra, San Juan, PR 00906; (787) 791-7750

Size: 5,780 acres

Closest Towns: The Forest is in the Carolina section of San Juan and just to the east of the tourism-centered Isla Verde and Condado.

The magnificent frigatebird soars over the ocean and plucks fish from near the water surface without ever landing. They are notorious for making other marine birds drop their prey, which the frigate catches before it hits the water.
BRUCE HALLETT

CARIBBEAN NATIONAL FOREST
(SITES 13, 14, 15, AND 16)

13. EL PORTAL

Description: The well-designed visitor center in the midst of the forest provides interpretive displays and viewing of tree ferns, cecropia trees, and other rain forest plants from a paved sidewalk, suitable for wheelchairs.

Viewing Information: Wildlife viewing at the visitor center is best in early morning when the birds are most active and calling. Commonly seen birds include red-legged thrush, gray and loggerhead kingbirds, bananaquit, black-whiskered vireo, Puerto Rican bullfinch, black-cowled oriole, stripe-headed tanager, and Puerto Rican woodpecker. The lizard cuckoo is often heard in the day and the Puerto Rican screech owl at night. In the morning and evening and after rains, the common coqui calls from amongst the leaves while several species of anolis lizards scamper on the tree trunks catching insects. Occasionally the endangered Puerto Rican boa is observed at night in the trees around and in the visitor center.

Directions: *From San Juan, take Highway 3 about 35 miles east to Hwy 191 (watch for the sign "El Yunque Rainforest" and "Bosque Nacional"). Travel 2.7 miles south on Hwy 191 to the clearly marked visitor center.*

Ownership: USDA National Forest Service, Caribbean National Forest, P.O. Box 490, Palmer, PR 00721; (787) 766-5335

Size: The Caribbean National Forest includes 28,000 acres of land.

Closest Towns: The small town of Luquillo is 9 miles east on Highway 3. San Juan is 35 miles west.

The lizard cuckoo is more often seen than heard as it moves through the forest hunting anolis lizards.
JOSÉ COLÓN

14. ANGELITO TRAIL

Description: The trail winds for 0.5 mile gently downhill to some large pools on the usually clear Río Mameyes. The peculiar canopy structure of the surrounding forest is the result of gradual recovery from the effects of several recent devastating hurricanes which ripped most of the smaller branches off the trees. Cecropia, recognized by its large silvery-bottomed leaves, is very fast growing and has rapidly filled in the many gaps in the canopy. The pomarrosa is common along streams and its fragrant, yellowish fruits can sometimes be found on the trail.

Viewing Information: This trail is one of Puerto Rico's most easily accessible areas in which to see ruddy quail-doves. Also present are Puerto Rican lizard cuckoos and many wintering warblers, such as northern parula and black-throated blue warblers. In the winter months, Louisiana waterthrushes are commonly found along the edge of Highway 988. The pretty yellow- and brown-striped sharp-mouthed lizard is common in this area. Mountain mullet, gobies, and several species of freshwater shrimp are readily evident in the river pools.

Directions: *From San Juan, take Hwy 3 about 35 miles east to Hwy 191 (watch for the sign "El Yunque Rainforest" and "Bosque Nacional"). Travel south on Hwy 191 to the intersection of Hwy 988 then drive east 2.8 miles to the trailhead. The highway crosses Río Mameyes just before the trailhead.*

Ownership: USDA Forest Service, Caribbean National Forest, P.O. Box 490, Palmer, PR 00721; (787) 766-5335

Size: The Caribbean National Forest includes 28,000 acres of land.

Closest Towns: The small town of Luquillo is 9 miles east on Hwy 3. San Juan is 35 miles west.

The ruddy quail-dove lives in dense forests and nests in bushes or low trees. The mournful coo is heard more often than the bird is seen.
JOSÉ COLÓN

HURRICANES: ILL WINDS THAT SHAPE CARIBBEAN WILDLIFE COMMUNITIES

by Joseph M. Wunderle, Jr.

The destructive force and frequent occurrence of hurricanes in the Caribbean plays a major role in shaping the habitats and composition of island wildlife communities. With winds exceeding 100 miles per hour, leaving a swath of destruction up to 100 miles wide, it's easy to imagine the substantial impact of hurricanes on Caribbean wildlife populations. The most obvious direct effect of hurricanes is death from exposure to high winds, rains, or wave action. Although various sea birds, shorebirds, herons, and egrets can die during a hurricane, terrestrial wildlife is affected more in the wake of the storm due to the damage it has wrought.

Bird studies in Puerto Rico and the Virgin Islands have found that nectarivores, frugivores, and seedeaters are most susceptible to population declines after hurricanes, since hurricane winds strip flowers, fruits, seeds, and leaves from plants. Many insectivore populations might be buffered from hurricane-induced food shortages by relying on insects which are mostly immune to hurricane effects. Predators fare better after hurricanes, as they can take advantage of the absence of cover to capture their prey, many of which may be forced to wander widely in search of food.

Nests, nesting sites, roosting sites, and nesting material can be destroyed by hurricanes. Species requiring large, old trees for nesting or roosting are particularly susceptible to hurricane effects, as these trees are the most vulnerable to damage. This is especially true for species such as the Puerto Rican parrot, which relies on cavities in old trees.

Not all population declines following hurricanes are attributed to mortality, as many species will migrate or wander into less-damaged habitats after storms. In fact, it is not unusual to find population increases in some undamaged habitats, particularly if the sites are rich in food. Therefore the ability to use a variety of disturbed habitats is key to survival of terrestrial wildlife in the wake of a hurricane.

Hurricanes leave tropical forests shockingly brown and leafless. But within a few weeks trees and vines begin to leaf out again. Openings in the canopy are quickly filled in by fast-growing, shade-intolerant species like the Cecropia.
RICARDO GARCIA

Description: The tower provides a view of the forest canopy and distant scenic vistas all the way to the Atlantic coast on a clear day. The Big Tree Trail winds through some of the best examples of tabonuco rain forest still existing in Puerto Rico and has interpretive signs for the first 0.3 mile.

Viewing Information: From the tower, red-tailed hawks, Puerto Rican broad-winged hawks, and black swifts are often evident. The elevation of the tower makes it possible to see many canopy-dwelling birds such as the Antillean euphonia, black-whiskered vireo, and more rarely, the endangered Puerto Rican parrot. On the trail, careful observation will reveal Puerto Rican todies, bananaquits, scaly-naped pigeons, and stripe-headed and Puerto Rican tanagers. Look for large forest snails and walking sticks, the aptly named insect, along the trail. Tall, slim sierra palms, cecropia with their large leaves with silver undersides, and pink-flowered *Tabebuia* are some of the common plants here. Freshwater gobies and shrimp are easily seen at stream crossings.

Directions: From San Juan, take Highway 3 about 35 miles east to Hwy 191 (watch for the sign "El Yunque Rainforest" and "Bosque Nacional"). Travel 5.6 miles south on Hwy 191 to the Yokahú viewing tower. The Big Tree trailhead to La Mina Falls is 0.9 mile beyond the viewing tower. From the falls, you can follow the La Mina Stream on a trail to the Palo Colorado Picnic Area and complete the circle by walking down Hwy 191 back to the trailhead.

Ownership: USDA Forest Service, Caribbean National Forest, P.O. Box 490, Palmer, PR 00721; (787) 766-5335

Size: The Caribbean National Forest includes 28,000 acres of land.

Closest Towns: The small town of Luquillo is 9 miles east on Hwy 3. San Juan is 35 miles west.

Walking sticks are common but not usually noticed members of the abundant and diverse insect fauna.
JOSÉ COLÓN

Description: These trails pass through extensive forests of sierra palms and cloud forest. Passing clouds envelop the forest in cool fog; then the clouds pass and the sun shines brilliantly again.

Viewing Information: Along the trails, Puerto Rican tanagers, todies, and pearly-eyed thrashers are common. This high-altitude forest is the home of the rare endemic elfin woods warbler. Several types of anole lizards are found on the vegetation, including the Puerto Rican giant anole. The small frogs in the genus *Eleutherodactylus*, called coqui, are represented in the cloud forest by the burrow coqui, whose call sounds like someone running their fingernail over a comb.

Directions: *From San Juan, take Highway 3 about 35 miles east to Hwy 191 (watch for the sign "El Yunque Rainforest" and "Bosque Nacional"). Travel 8.3 miles south on Hwy 191 to the intersection of forest road 9938 then turn right 0.2 mile to the trailhead. The Mount Britton Lookout Tower is about 1.2 miles up the trail, which continues and joins the El Yunque Trail to the lookout tower at the summit of El Yunque.*

About 250 yards past the gate which stops vehicular traffic on Hwy 191, the Tradewinds Trail departs from the road to the right and meanders about 4 miles to the peak of El Toro. The trail continues as El Toro Trail about 2.2 miles to intersect Hwy 186 on the west side of the forest.

Ownership: USDA Forest Service, Caribbean National Forest, P.O. Box 490, Palmer, PR 00721; (787) 766-5335

Size: The Caribbean National Forest includes 28,000 acres of land.

Closest Towns: The small town of Luquillo is 9 miles east on Hwy 3. San Juan is 35 miles west.

NORTHEAST PUERTO RICO AND EASTERN ISLANDS

The tree ferns in the foreground are common on moist upland sites, but the distant view shown is often obscured by low clouds. JOSÉ COLÓN

Description: This nature reserve has something for everyone: a beach, good snorkeling, scenic vistas, a boardwalk through a mangrove forest, a historic lighthouse, and one of the best bioluminescent lagoons in the world. The bioluminescence is produced by microscopic organisms which produce sparkles of light when jostled. Reservations are required and visitors must travel with guided tours unless entering by boat or kayak.

Viewing Information: The boardwalk provides views and interpretive signs of all four species of mangroves, fish, crabs, birds, and the bioluminescent lagoon. Schools of huge mullet meander in the shallows while tarpon and barracuda lurk in the shade of the boardwalk. The crater nests of tilapia are active from February until August. The sound of a feeding snook—a "slurk," like a sucking splash—is often heard in the mangroves along the edge of open water. Shallow waters and exposed mud flats are inhabited by blue, mangrove, and fiddler crabs which provide food for many shorebirds, night herons, and green herons. The tropical dry forest on the uplands has mongooses and green iguanas more than three feet long. It's the winter home of many neotropical migrant birds. Red-tailed hawks patrol the forest while ospreys, frigatebirds, and pelicans feed in the lagoon and along the shoreline. From the elevation of a patio at the lighthouse, brown boobies and tropicbirds can often be seen in the winter. In the summer, several species of gulls and terns nest in the area.

Directions: From Fajardo, take Highway 987 north five miles toward Las Croabas and past El Conquistador Hotel. The entrance to the refuge is marked with a sign on the left. An admission fee is charged.

Ownership: Conservation Trust of Puerto Rico, P.O. Box 9023554, San Juan, PR 00902-3554; (787) 722-5882. Reservations are required for admission.

Size: 440 acres

Closest Towns: The small town of Fajardo five miles to the south can provide most tourist needs. Metropolitan San Juan is 35 miles to the west on Hwy 3.

The oldest rocks of the reserve are of volcanic origin and date from the upper Cretaceous period about 100 million years ago. Indians used the Cabezas as a landmark signaling the northeastern shores of Borinquen. In pre-Columbian times, the reserve was covered with trees, and its native wildlife—including birds, reptiles, fish, and crustaceans—served as a source of food. Artifacts of the Igneri culture, a group that migrated through the Lesser Antilles at the beginning of the Christian era, have been found on the reserve.

RICARDO MEDINA

18. LA CORDILLERA NATURE RESERVE

Description: La Cordillera is a group of rocks and islands off the northeast coast of Puerto Rico, with dozens of good dive sites. Cayo Lobos snorkel site is a steep slope that extends from the surface to a sand bottom at about 20 feet on the protected west side of the island. Cayo Diablo scuba site is a coral- and sponge-covered steep slope from 40 to 60 feet deep, off the west and south shores of the cay.

Viewing Information: At the Cayo Lobos snorkel site, the wall is composed of very large brain corals along with many other species of coral, sea fans, and sponges. It is particularly noted for its cleaning sites, where brightly colored gobies wait to pick parasites from large fish, especially grouper, blue tang, French and gray angels, and many species of parrotfish. The deeper water of Cayo Diablo reef is frequented by graceful stingrays and hawksbill turtles, both of which have become accustomed to divers. Queen triggerfish, yellowtail snapper, barracuda, and other species of reef fish are commonly seen. This is also a good area to view sea birds while traveling to and from the dive sites. Brown pelicans, brown boobies, and magnificent frigatebirds are present year-round. Noddy, sooty, royal, bridled, and roseate terns are present from May to September, and tropicbirds are present from October to April. Camping is permitted on Icacos and the cays. Day use of Palominitos is allowed.

Directions: *Most visitors rely on tour operators. Most of the dive operators who offer snorkeling and/or scuba diving trips to La Cordillera are based on the coast, north or south of Fajardo.*

Ownership: Puerto Rico Department of Natural and Environmental Resources owns most of the islands. Two of the islands, Palominos and Cayo Lobos, are privately owned. Land access is not needed to dive.

Size: The islands vary in size from 20 acres to mere exposed rocks, but the marine park area is 46 square miles of ocean and less than a square mile of land, of which 224 acres is publicly owned.

Closest Town: Fajardo

NORTHEAST PUERTO RICO AND EASTERN ISLANDS

Queen triggerfish are quite common on Caribbean reefs where they eat crabs, sea urchins, and other invertebrates. Their tough leathery skin protects them from retaliation by their prey.
STEVE SIMONSEN

Description: The diverse habitats in the refuge include subtropical dry forest on the Mount Resaca unit, coastal mangroves at Puerto de Manglar, grass-covered Flamenco Peninsula, and a variety of cays with surf-swept shorelines and sedge-vegetated uplands. Snorkelers and scuba divers can explore beautiful coral reefs in waters adjacent to refuge lands.

Viewing Information: Hawksbill turtles nest on the island beaches year-round with a peak in activity from July through November. Leatherback turtles deposit their eggs April to July on sandy beaches which have easy access to deep water. Winter breeding birds include brown boobies, red-footed boobies, masked boobies, red-billed tropicbirds, and white-tailed tropicbirds. About 60,000 sooty terns nest in May on Flamenco Peninsula, along with noddy terns, bridled terns, roseate terns, sandwich terns, and Audubon shearwaters. Landing on the cays other than Cayo Luís Peña and Isla Culebrita requires a special use permit from the refuge manager.

Directions: *Culebra is about 17 miles east of Puerto Rico and 12 miles west of St. Thomas. Daily commercial flights are available from Isla Grande and Fajardo Airports in Puerto Rico and from St. Thomas. A passenger ferry travels from Fajardo to Culebra daily.*

Ownership: U.S. Fish and Wildlife Service, Culebra, PR 00775; (787) 742-0115

Size: The 1,568 acres of the refuge encompass various tracts on the main island and all the adjacent small cays except Cayo Del Norte.

Closest Town: Small hotels, guest houses, and restaurants are available in the village of Dewey.

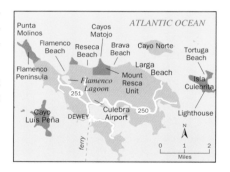

Masked boobies forage for flying fish far out of sight of land, but pairs return annually to the same nest site on the ground.

DAVID W. NELLIS

20. BAHÍA PUERTO MOSQUITO NATURE RESERVE

Description: The nature reserve includes some well-developed coastal mangrove communities, several cays, and some delightful swimming beaches. The star attraction is the dense populations of bioluminescent dinoflagellates which can be seen at night in Bahía Puerto Mosquito.

Viewing Information: The phosphorescent bay is most easily observed from the commercial tour boats, but wading or swimming in the bay is more exciting. Dinoflagellates, a species of microscopic plankton, individually illuminate themselves when disturbed or jostled. Moving your hand through the water leaves a sparkling wake. The dinoflagellates are best appreciated on moonless nights. Three to five days after the full moon, it is dark from sundown until moonrise at 10 or 11 P.M. Balneario Sun Bay is a long, beautiful arm of water which provides swimming and snorkeling. Palometa are common in the wave break zone while mojarra, a silvery fish with a deeply forked tail, and lizardfish feed over the open sand.

Directions: The ferry from Fajardo lands at Isabel Segunda. Then take Highway 997 south to Esperanza. If you arrive at the airport, take Hwy 200 toward Isabel Segunda until you reach the intersection with Hwy 201. Follow Hwy 201 south to Esperanza. Tour boats leave for Bahía Puerto Mosquito most evenings from the town dock in Esperanza. Alternatively, you can leave Esperanza and drive toward Isabel Segunda about 1.7 miles and turn south on a short dirt road that ends at Bahía Puerto Mosquito.

Ownership: Puerto Rico Department of Natural and Environmental Resources, P.O. Box 9066600, Puerta de Tierra, San Juan, PR 00906; (787) 741-8683

Size: 1,190 acres

Closest Towns: Esperanza is immediately adjacent to the site; the larger Isabel Segunda is about 5 miles to the northeast.

Description: The U.S. Navy owns nearly two-thirds of Vieques Island, with a training facility and maneuvering areas on the east and the Naval Ammunition Detachment to the west. The Laguna Kiani Boardwalk provides an opportunity to pleasantly view a mangrove ecosystem at close range.

Viewing Information: The boardwalk allows one to walk comfortably through a mangrove forest with green herons and night herons roosting in the shadows and pelicans resting on top of the canopy. Great blue herons, little blue herons, great egrets, and snowy egrets feed in the shallow water of the lagoon. Many species of shorebirds such as ruddy turnstones and greater yellowlegs feed on exposed mud flats. Black-necked stilts nest on the edges of the mud flats and white-cheeked pintails lead their brood to the pond from nearby nests. The lagoon is inhabited by many species of juvenile fish, including snappers, grunts, and barracuda. When snorkeling off Green Beach you are likely to see the silvery mojarra, with their deeply forked tails, and whiskered goatfish over the sand, sergeant majors in mid-water, and squirrelfish, parrotfish, blue tang, and dusky damselfish among the coral.

Directions: *You can get to Vieques by air from San Juan or by ferry from Fajardo. Travel west from Isabel Segunda on Highway 200 until you reach the gate of the Naval Ammunition Support Detachment. Stop and get a pass; then continue west on a dirt road for about 4 miles past the gate. The Laguna Kiani Boardwalk is on the left just after a bridge. Green Beach is another mile west of the boardwalk on the same road. If you take the southernmost fork to a dead end, you can snorkel directly from the beach over an interesting shallow reef community.*

Ownership: United States Navy

Size: The naval ammunition facility (NAF) owns 8,000 acres on the west end of Vieques. Much of the land is closed to public use for security reasons.

Closest Town: Isabel Segunda is 9 miles east of Green Beach.

Goatfish seek small invertebrate prey while they probe in the sand using mobile finger-like appendages under their chin.

SUSAN SPECK

Description: This refuge is a series of diked ponds and lagoons with fresh, brackish, and salt water. Cattails and mangroves along the water's edge offer shelter to many birds.

Viewing Information: This is the best waterfowl viewing area in Puerto Rico. The white-cheeked pintail, West Indian whistling duck, common moorhen, American coot, Caribbean coot, and many species of herons and egrets are regularly seen feeding, roosting, and nesting in or near the ponds. Ruddy ducks, blue-winged teal, green-winged teal, and scaup regularly migrate to these ponds for the winter. Brown pelicans, magnificent frigatebirds, and over-wintering ospreys often fish in the lagoons. Fishermen catch tarpon, snook, tucunare, tilapia, and largemouth bass. The upland forest on the refuge is in-habited by Puerto Rican woodpeckers, cave swallows, and overwintering war-blers. A breeding population of yellow-crowned bishops, a bird introduced to Puerto Rico from Africa, is found in the marsh vegetation around the lagoons.

Directions: *From Humacao, take Highway 3 east toward Punta Santiago about 7 miles to the sign marking the refuge entrance near kilometer marker 74.3. From Fajardo, take Hwy 3 southwest 17 miles to Humacao Beach (Balneario de Humacao), with the small island Cayo Santiago just offshore. After the main en-trance to the beach, Hwy 3 turns inland for 0.9 mile to the refuge, on the left just past a small concrete bridge.*

Ownership: Puerto Rico Department of Natural and Environmental Resources P.O. Box 9066600, Puerta de Tierra, San Juan, PR 00906; (787) 852-6088

Size: 2,800 acres

Closest Towns: There are numerous small towns and villages along the road in either direction from the refuge.

NORTHEAST PUERTO RICO AND EASTERN ISLANDS

The West Indian whistling duck is nocturnal and most often seen at dawn and dusk as it travels to and from its forest roosts.
BRUCE HALLETT

PUERTO RICO CENTRAL MOUNTAINS

Lush green forests with peaks often shrouded in clouds, narrow twisting roads, the cultivation of coffee and bananas, and small towns characterize Puerto Rico's central mountains (or La Cordillera Central). Seven state forests are strung along this rugged mountain chain and offer excellent viewing opportunities, which include numerous lizard and coquís sightings. Additionally, birds such as the Puerto Rican emerald and green mango hummingbird, Antillean euphonia, ruddy quail-dove, and elfin woods warbler are denizens of the cloud forests.

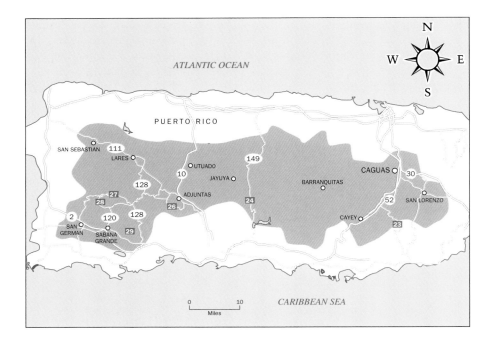

23. CARITE STATE FOREST

Description: This is a mountain forest where 85 inches of rainfall produces lush tropical vegetation, including thickets of large bamboo and decorative tree ferns. This modest block of forest shows remarkable biodiversity with 204 species of trees, many endemic birds, and a winter population of migrant birds from North America. A picnic and camping area with roofed shelters is near the main road and a nature trail winds through the forest to a large blue pool in a small stream.

Viewing Information: If you visit this forest early in the morning or at dusk, you'll be rewarded with a symphony of bird and frog calls. Broad-winged hawks, sharp-shinned hawks, scaly-naped pigeons, Puerto Rican todies, Puerto Rican woodpeckers, Puerto Rican bullfinches, Puerto Rican emerald and green mango hummingbirds, stripe-headed tanagers, and Antillean euphonia are among the many birds which may be seen in the forest. The seven species of the small but loud tree frogs, locally called coquí, are incited to calling contests by the slightest rain. The Puerto Rican racer and Puerto Rican boa are two of the common snakes in this forest.

Directions: *From San Juan, take Highway 52 south through Caguas. Six miles past Caguas exit, take Hwy 184 and turn left under the expressway. Then drive 6 miles to the forest entrance.*

Ownership: Puerto Rico Department of Natural and Environmental Resources P.O. Box 9066600, Puerta de Tierra, San Juan, PR 00906; (787) 747-4545

Size: 6,000 acres

Closest Towns: San Juan to the north or many small towns offering tourist amenities along the south coast.

The Puerto Rican tody is found in most upland forests and lowland thickets where it catches walking and flying insects with short flights from a perch. It nests in burrows on the face of banks.
GIFF BEATON

COQUÍS: LORDS OF THE NIGHT

by Rafael L. Joglar and Patricia A. Burrows

Coquí is the local name for a group of tree frogs that call melodiously at night. Coquís live throughout Puerto Rico and the Virgin Islands from mountain rain forests to dry lowlands and moist urban gardens. They are most active in humid habitats at night. The greatest diversity of species is found in the high-elevation rain forests such as El Yunque, Toro Negro, and Maricao with species living on the forest floor, in bromeliads, or in limestone cave formations.

No matter where you are in the Caribbean you will be able to hear their courtship calls on moist evenings. The call of the most common and widespread species is "KO-KEE," hence the name. Males call to declare their territory and attract females for mating.

Unlike the eggs of most other toads and frogs, coqui eggs hatch directly into small frogs after incubation in a moist terrestrial habitat. Coquís are nocturnal predators of insects and other small invertebrates and they are prey for many vertebrates and invertebrates. As with amphibians worldwide, coquís are very sensitive to environmental change and are showing a general decline in numbers. In the past three decades, three of the 16 species in Puerto Rico have probably become extinct.

The calls of the coquí are a trademark sound of Puerto Rican evenings in city and country alike. PETE CARMICHAEL

24. TORO NEGRO STATE FOREST

Description: The seven segments of this state forest are arrayed along Highway 143 as it winds through the forest along the spine of the central mountain range. The road passes just below the summit of Cerro Punta, the highest mountain in Puerto Rico at 4,388 feet.

Viewing Information: The area has some of the wettest rain forest in Puerto Rico and one of the few examples of cloud forest outside the Caribbean National Forest. The vegetation along the road varies with elevation but sierra palms, cecropia, and tree ferns are almost always in sight. Birds regularly seen include Puerto Rican flycatchers, Puerto Rican and green mango hummingbirds, Puerto Rican todies, Antillean euphonia, and ruddy quail-doves. Coquí are represented by eight species in this ideal habitat. The white-lipped frog's chorus of "*pink-pink-pink*" can be heard in the wettest spots. Three species of anole lizards scamper on the trees while a tiny gecko, which lives among the leaf litter, is surprisingly abundant. The Puerto Rican racer is seen along the trails. A map to the network of trails in the forest is available from the forest office.

Directions: *From Ponce, take Highway 10 north 20 miles and turn right on Hwy 143 (Ruta Panoramica, Puerto Rico's scenic route). Hwy 139 north from Ponce to Hwy 143 is a much slower, winding road—an alternative with better scenery. Hwy 143 passes through several segments of the forest before reaching the headquarters at kilometer marker 32.4.*

Ownership: Puerto Rico Department of Natural and Environmental Resources, P.O. Box 9066600, Puerta de Tierra, San Juan, PR 00906; (787) 721-5495

Size: 6,945 acres

Closest Towns: Ponce is 20 miles to the south; Arecibo is 50 miles to the north.

PUERTO RICO CENTRAL MOUNTAINS

The Puerto Rican brown racer is a quick snake often seen momentarily as it slithers out of site into thick vegetation.
TOMÁS A. CARLO

53

25. RIO ABAJO STATE FOREST

Description: This wet forest has developed on a karst landscape with over 80 inches of rain per year. Mahogany and teak trees have been planted in some of the valleys, while native plants form a more diverse community on the hillsides. The lowlands have huge, impenetrable clumps of giant bamboo. The road is scenic, narrow, and winding with almost no traffic.

Viewing Information: The Antillean euphonia and Puerto Rican lizard cuckoo are more often heard than seen in the thick vegetation. The stripe-headed tanager and ruddy quail-dove are regularly present along the trails and broad-winged hawks call while soaring over the forest. The calling of coquís is most conspicuous at dawn and dusk and after rains, but it is a real challenge to see one of these secretive, well-camouflaged tree frogs. Lizards include seven species of anoles and two geckos along with the Puerto Rican boa and Puerto Rican brown racer. In the evening, the 13 species of bats thoroughly patrol the forest and carry on twittered arguments as they feed on fruit, flowers, and insects.

Directions: *From Arecibo, take Highway 10 south toward Utuado and exit at Hwy 621; then turn right to continue. The office headquarters is 1.4 miles on your left. Another 2 miles brings you to a picnic area and restrooms. If you continue another mile or so, a nice trail signed "Vereda Santa Rosa" departs from the pavement 100 yards before the gate. The trail is a road that is passable for about 1.5 miles before the rocks begin to scrape the bottom of a low car.*

Ownership: Puerto Rico Department of Natural and Environmental Resources, P.O. Box 9066600, Puerta de Tierra, San Juan, PR 00906; (787) 880-6557

Size: 5,780 acres

Closest Towns: The small town of Utuado and the more cosmopolitan Arecibo are almost equidistant, in opposite directions on Hwy 10.

Tiny Sphaerodactylus *geckos do not climb trees but forage on and in the leaf litter on the forest floor.*
DAVID W. NELLIS

26. GUILARTE STATE FOREST

Description: Highway 518, Puerto Rico's scenic route (Ruta Panorámica), winds through the wet forest of the central mountains, providing good mountain birding and excellent scenic vistas. With an elevation of 2,500 to 3,900 feet and 90 inches of rainfall per year, the air is usually cool and moist. The forest property is dispersed into six sites along the road.

Viewing Information: This is one of the best sites to view the high-forest-dwelling sharp-shinned and broad-winged hawks as they perch on roadside lookouts. The colorful Puerto Rican tody, green mango hummingbird, Antillean euphonia, Puerto Rican tanager, and stripe-headed tanager can be seen in the understory vegetation, while ruddy quail-doves feed on the forest floor and are reluctant to fly at all. Four species of coquís are present along with five species of tree-dwelling anole lizards. The well-camouflaged Puerto Rican boa is seldom recognized, except when it is spotted crossing a road or trail.

Directions: *From Ponce, take Highway 10 north 12 miles to the junction with Hwy 518. Turn left on Hwy 518 and travel 5 miles to the visitor center. Hwy 518 is a narrow, winding road in the mountains with little traffic and many chances to view wildlife. A left fork at the visitor center becomes a single-lane road through mostly undisturbed forest and ends at the beginning of a foot trail.*

Ownership: Puerto Rico Department of Natural and Environmental Resources, P.O. Box 9066600, Puerta de Tierra, San Juan, PR 00906; (787) 724-3724 (San Juan) or (787) 844-4660 (Ponce)

Size: 6,304 acres

Closest Towns: The small town of Adjuntas is nearby while the large city of Ponce is on the coast to the south.

The Antillean or blue-headed euphonia is a tanager more commonly seen than heard in the upland forest which it inhabits.
TOMÁS A. CARLO

Description: The hatchery is a series of ponds and pools supplied with a constant flow of fresh water. The meticulously maintained grounds and paved walkways occupy a civilized pocket in the flowering forest on the adjacent hillsides. The hatchery is reached via a winding drive along the Rio Maricao.

Viewing Information: The clear water in the ponds provides excellent views of the native and introduced fish raised in the hatchery. The dajao, a native catadromus fish, is difficult to find in the wild but easily observed in the pools. The hatchery produces largemouth bass, several species of tilapia, and redear sunfish for stocking ponds and lakes. Also on exhibit are tarpon and pacú, a sport fish from Venezuela. The black-cowled oriole, hummingbirds, Puerto Rican woodpecker, and a variety of warblers live in the surrounding forest.

Directions: From Mayagüez, take Highway 105 east to the town of Maricao; then turn right on Hwy 410 which leads to the fish hatchery. From Ponce, travel west on Hwy 2 and turn north on Hwy 120 to Hwy 410 in Maricao. Travel 1 mile on Hwy 410 winding through the forest until the road ends at the fish hatchery's Los Viveros parking lot.

Ownership: Puerto Rico Department of Natural and Environmental Resources, P.O. Box 9066600, Puerta de Tierra, San Juan, PR 00906; (787) 851-7297

Size: 50 acres

Closest Towns: Mayagüez, Ponce, and the small village of Maricao.

Largemouth bass are a popular and prolific freshwater game fish which have been stocked in many freshwater impoundments in Puerto Rico and the Virgin Islands.
THE STATE OF FLORIDA GAME AND FISH

28. MARICAO STATE FOREST

Description: This is one of the best examples of wet mountain forest and cloud forest remaining in Puerto Rico. Along Highway 120, a large stone observation tower with interior stairs allows visitors to see over the tree canopy for sweeping vistas toward the south and west coast and to Cabo Rojo over 20 miles away. These high mountain forests near Maricao provide the shade and habitat needed for growing coffee shrubs. The village of Maricao celebrates with a coffee festival in February.

Viewing Information: The recently discovered elfin woods warbler may be seen in the higher elevation cloud forest. On the trails in the forest, bridled quail-doves rustle in the leaf litter and many hummingbirds, including the Puerto Rican green mango, feed on the abundant flowering trees. Also regularly seen or heard are the stripe-headed tanager, lesser Antillean pewee, loggerhead kingbird, Puerto Rican woodpecker, Puerto Rican vireo, Antillean euphonia, and lizard cuckoo.

Directions: *At Mayagüez, exit Hwy 2 at Calle Mendez Vigo and turn east. The street becomes Hwy 106, which you should follow to Hwy 119 and turn right. Then turn left on Hwy 105 to the junction with Hwy 120 just south of Maricao. Hwy 105 between Maricao and Mayagüez is a more scenic route but should be traveled only in a westerly direction as the beginning of the road is difficult to find in Mayagüez, due to lack of signs.*

Ownership: Puerto Rico Department of Natural and Environmental Resources, P.O. Box 9066600, Puerta de Tierra, San Juan, PR 00906; (787) 721-5495

Size: 10,569 acres

Closest Towns: The village of Maricao is adjacent to the forest. The small town of San German is 20 miles to the south and the large town of Mayagüez is 25 miles to the west.

The elfin woods warblers are only found in the high elevation dwarf forest of Puerto Rico. They are very active and move rapidly about as they forage on insects from leaves and twigs.
GIFF BEATON

Description: This forest lies in the transition zone between the low-elevation dry forest of Guánica and the humid forest of the mountains such as Maricao and Toro Negro. Elevations range from 250 to 1,500 feet. The underlying serpentine rock yields thin, poor soils with stunted trees, except along watercourses. Over 150 species of trees have been recorded in the forest. Notable species include brittle thatchpalm, violet tree, Florida fiddlewood, and María.

Viewing Information: Birds of interest in the forest include the plain pigeon, Puerto Rican woodpecker, Puerto Rican bullfinch, Puerto Rican lizard cuckoo, Puerto Rican tody, and ruddy quail-dove. The red reflective eyes of the endangered Puerto Rican nightjar aid in finding it in the dark. Several species of anolis lizards scamper up and down the tree trunks and seven species of coquís call after rains and in the evening. The Puerto Rican racer is active by day while the Puerto Rican boa is more frequently seen at night.

Directions: *From Ponce, take Highway 2 west toward Mayagüez. Exit Hwy 2 on Hwy 102 at Sabana Grande. From Sabana Grande, take Hwy 368 west to kilometer 2.1; then turn north. The office, recreation facilities, and trailheads are marked with signs just north of Hwy 368.*

Ownership: Puerto Rico Department of Natural and Environmental Resources, P.O. Box 9066600, Puerta de Tierra, San Juan, PR 00906; (787) 721-5495

Size: 3,341 acres

Closest Towns: Sabana Grande and Yauco. Larger towns with more tourist amenities are Guánica and San Germán.

Anolis gundlachi *scampers up and down tree trunks with great agility as it catches insects.* TOMÁS A. CARLO

PUERTO RICO SOUTH COAST

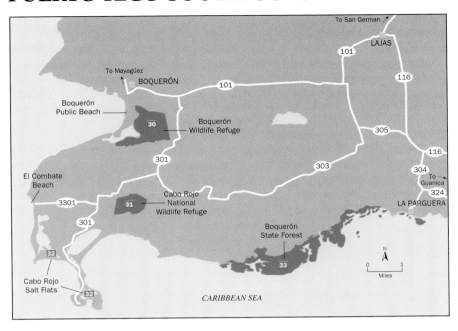

To San German

LAJAS

101

116

To Mayagüez

BOQUERÓN

101

Boquerón
Public Beach

30

Boquerón
Wildlife Refuge

305

116

301

303

304

El Combate
Beach

3301

31

Cabo Rojo
National
Wildlife Refuge

301

Boquerón
State Forest

To
Guanica

324

LA PARGUERA

N

0   1
Miles

32

33

Cabo Rojo
Salt Flats

32

CARIBBEAN SEA

30. BOQUERÓN WILDLIFE REFUGE

Description: This mangrove-fringed, brackish lagoon provides good viewing of wetland birds and is also popular with anglers. The refuge was established in 1963 as mitigation for the loss of other lagoons in the area to agricultural development. Mangroves are the most abundant plant followed by salt-resistant cattails. Ruppia, a submerged weed growing in the open waters, is highly favored by ducks as a food source.

Viewing Information: More than 130 species of birds have been recorded on the refuge. A flock of brown pelicans roosts in the mangroves as do 150 black-crowned night herons. Ruddy duck, Caribbean coot, pied-billed grebe, least grebe, and the endangered yellow-shouldered blackbird all nest in the refuge. Tarpon, ladyfish, and snook are trophy targets of fishermen while the abundant tilapia and catfish are caught for the table. Hunting for blue-winged teal, common moorhen, and common snipe is allowed in the refuge from November through January. Exploring the meandering mangrove channels by canoe, kayak, or small boat is encouraged.

Directions: *From Mayagüez, travel south 3 miles on Highway 2; then exit on Hwy 100 to the southwest. After 12 miles, Hwy 100 terminates at Hwy 101. Travel east on Hwy 101 to Las Arenas, then south 0.7 mile on Hwy 301 to the refuge entrance on the west side of the road.*

Ownership: Puerto Rico Department of Natural and Environmental Resources, HC-01, Box 1000, Boquerón, PR 00622-9701; (787) 851-4795

Size: 463 acres

Closest Towns: The village of Boquerón provides most tourist needs. The city of Mayagüez has more comprehensive shopping.

Great Egrets are the largest of the white, long-legged wading birds in the Caribbean. They stand and wait or stride sedately while searching for small fish.
DAVID W. NELLIS

31. CABO ROJO NATIONAL WILDLIFE REFUGE

Description: The refuge was a listening post for the Foreign Broadcast Information Service until 1974, when the property was transferred to the U.S. Fish and Wildlife Service. It is now the headquarters for the Caribbean National Wildlife Refuge, which has a visitor center with several good displays. Much of the land has been heavily grazed in the past with the result that biodiversity is limited but increasing as succession progresses. Two blinds allow observations at seasonal ponds, and numerous trails and roads allow pedestrian access throughout the refuge.

Viewing Information: The brushy vegetation provides winter habitat for many neotropical migrant warblers from the continental United States and Canada. Local species regularly observed on the trails include black-faced grassquits, bananaquits, ground doves, and smooth-billed anis. Soaring overhead are turkey vultures, red-tailed hawks, and occasionally an osprey, merlin, or peregrine falcon. Small Indian mongooses have established significant populations in and around the refuge. Introduced patas monkeys inhabit the adjacent Sierra Bermeja mountains and are known to pass through the refuge. Wildlife abundance is often keyed to the ecological conditions which follow the rains in the fall.

Directions: *Take Highway 101 east from Boquerón 1.7 miles to Las Arenas. Turn right on Hwy 301 and drive 3.2 miles to the refuge entrance sign with a yellow-shouldered blackbird. Follow the entrance road about 0.8 mile to the headquarters and visitor center.*

Ownership: U.S. Fish and Wildlife Service, P.O. Box 510, Boquerón, PR; (787) 851-7258

Size: 587 acres

Closest Towns: The village of Boquerón offers lodging and restaurants. The modern city of Mayagüez is about 12 miles north.

PUERTO RICO SOUTH COAST

Ospreys use their long talons to catch fish up to 2 pounds in weight near the water surface.
JOSÉ COLÓN

61

32. CABO ROJO SALT FLATS

Description: This coastal lagoon has been the source for commercial evaporative salt production for centuries. The natural ecosystem remains intact and produces scenic beauty and solitude not found in any other area of coastal Puerto Rico. On a hill south of the lagoons is the Cabo Rojo historic lighthouse.

Viewing Information: Migratory shorebirds are present in great numbers from September to November and this is a likely spot to see a piping plover or a snowy plover. Herons and egrets are seen in more variable numbers year-round along with the occasional flamingo. Flocks of white-cheeked pintails are often seen on the pond. In the adjacent woodlands, Caribbean martins swoop above the trees catching insects, while yellow-shouldered blackbirds hunt insects in the brush and the rare lizard *Anolis cookii* catches insects on the tree trunks.

Directions: *From Ponce, take Highway 2 west and exit on Hwy 116 south, then travel about 12 miles until you reach Hwy 305 and turn left. After 1.6 miles, turn right on Hwy 303, then left on Hwy 101, and left again on Hwy 301. From Mayagüez, take Hwy 2 south and exit on Hwy 100 south. Follow it about 8 miles to the flashing light at Hwy 101. Turn left on Hwy 101, then right on Hwy 301. Do not take Hwy 3301 to Combate Beach but continue on Hwy 301 until the pavement ends in the salt flats. You can drive along the lagoon to the salt production facility and park at the base of the hill that supports the lighthouse. Watch out for muddy spots and soft sand.*

Ownership: The salt flats are privately owned and the area immediately adjacent to the lighthouse is part of the Boquerón State Forest.

Size: Approximately 1,000 acres of lagoons and salt flats, plus 500 acres of upland.

Closest Towns: The small fishing village of Combate is the closest community. The small coastal town of Boquerón is 8 miles to the north.

The snowy plover is most often found on isolated mud flats with crystallized salt.
TOMÁS A. CARLO

Description: This is one of seven state forests established in 1918. The forest is divided into eight sections and contains mangrove, salt flat, coastal plain, and island ecosystems. A very pleasant boardwalk winding through the coastal mangroves to the open sea is accessible from the village of Boquerón.

Viewing Information: The coastal mangroves and nearby shallow waters provide roosting and nesting for pelicans, West Indian whistling ducks, white-crowned pigeons, and night herons. Black-necked stilts, American oyster-catchers, greater yellowlegs, piping plovers, and other shorebirds feed on the shallow mud flats. Summer sea bird migrants feeding in coastal waters include least tern, roseate tern, royal tern, black tern, and laughing gull. The best way to view waterbirds is to ease along the edges of mangroves in a kayak, canoe, or small boat. The endangered endemic yellow-shouldered blackbird is found on the nearby brushy uplands.

Directions: *From Mayagüez, travel south on Highway 2 to Hwy 100, which road signs show as "Cabo Rojo." Follow Hwy 100 south 12 miles and turn right on Hwy 101 into the village of Boquerón. Turn right at the waterfront and after you pass Club Nautico you can see the forest headquarters on your right. From Ponce, take Hwy 2 west about 20 miles, exit on Hwy 116 and travel about 8 miles southwest to Hwy 305. Follow Hwy 305 and turn right onto Hwy 303, then left onto Hwy 101, and on to Boquerón.*

Ownership: Puerto Rico Department of Natural and Environmental Resources, P.O. Box 9066600, Puerta de Tierra, San Juan, PR 00906; (787) 851-7260

Size: 4,776 acres

Closest Towns: The town of Boquerón has small hotels, restaurants, and gift shops. The cities of San German and Mayagüez offer more comprehensive services.

Black-necked stilts forage for marine invertebrates living in shallow muddy bottoms. Stilts usually associate in flocks and call with a penetrating wit-wit-wit when disturbed.
DAVID W. NELLIS

PUERTO RICO SOUTH COAST

34. LA PARGUERA NATURE RESERVE

Description: This reserve was formed to protect the mangrove communities and two bays in particular, which have populations of microscopic, bioluminescent dinoflagellates.

Viewing Information: Each of the tiny plankton organisms called dinoflagellates floating in the water briefly turns on its chemically-powered light when disturbed. A hand drawn through the water leaves a phosphorescent wake and a swimming fish leaves a brilliant trail like a meteor. The dinoflagellates can only be seen at night. A moonless sky makes them even more dramatic. By day, this area is one of the largest coastal mangrove communities in Puerto Rico with four species of mangroves. Snorkeling along the outer edge of the mangroves allows you to see many of the juvenile reef fish which take refuge in the mangrove roots before moving to the reefs as adults. Also present along the mangroves and the adjacent upland vegetation are brown pelicans, shorebirds, white-crowned pigeons, troupials, and the endangered yellow-shouldered blackbird.

Directions: *Take Highway 2 west about 20 miles from Ponce towards Mayagüez. Exit on Hwy 116 and follow it south and west 12 miles to Hwy 304. Follow Hwy 304 south to the village of La Parguera. Tour boats to the phosphorescent bay leave every evening from the dock at La Parguera, except for some holidays.*

Ownership: Puerto Rico Department of Natural and Environmental Resources, P.O. Box 9066600, Puerta de Tierra, San Juan, PR 00906; (787) 724-3724

Size: 12,628 acres

Closest Towns: The village of La Parguera can take care of most tourist needs. The larger town of Guánica provides more shopping variety.

Sponge- and invertebrate-encrusted mangrove roots provide food and protection for juveniles of many species of reef fish. STEVE SIMONSEN

35. GUÁNICA STATE FOREST

Description: A world biosphere reserve, Guánica is one of the best examples of subtropical dry forest in the United States, and is widely considered to be the best birding site in Puerto Rico.

Viewing Information: Eleven of the 14 endemic Puerto Rican birds can be found in this forest. Over 700 species of plants have been recorded, including 48 which are endangered and 16 which are only found in the forest. The best time for birding is from first light to an hour or so after sunrise, then again in the hour before dark. Puerto Rican todies, troupials, mangrove cuckoos, Adelaide's warblers, and Puerto Rican bullfinches are evident along Highway 334 and the 40 kilometers of trails. Almost the entire population of the endangered Puerto Rican nightjar is in the forest and one of the few breeding sites of the endangered Puerto Rican toad is near Tamarindo Beach. An offshore cay called Gilligan's Island has a ferry service and makes an interesting day trip. If you snorkel from the low wooden platform on the north side of the island, you will pass over shallow sea grass, coral rubble, and sand flats with starfish, sea cucumbers, and parrotfish. As you continue around Gilligan's Island, you'll pass through a channel with juveniles of many species of reef fish taking shelter among the mangrove stilt roots.

Directions: *From Ponce, take Hwy 2 west 20 miles, then go south on Hwy 116. After 2.5 miles, turn left and follow Hwy 334 through the forest to the headquarters and visitor center. For the Gilligan's Island launch, take Hwy 333 past the Copamarina resort and turn right at the "Mary Lee's" sign.*

Ownership: Puerto Rico Department of Natural and Environmental Resources, P.O. Box 9066600, Puerta de Tierra, San Juan, PR 00906; (787) 721-5495

Size: 9,900 acres

Closest Towns: Hwy 2 goes to Ponce to the east or Mayagüez to the west. A resort hotel, guest houses, and several restaurants are located along the beach and in the nearby village of Guánica.

The mangrove cuckoo is often heard in the breeding season and just before a rain but is difficult to spot due to its inclination to slink silently through the foliage.
JOSÉ COLÓN

36. CAJA DE MUERTOS (COFFIN ISLAND) NATURE RESERVE

Description: The two-mile-long island is named for the coffin-like silhouette it presents when viewed from the hills above Ponce or from a ship at sea. An elegant lighthouse is perched on the highest part of the coffin at an elevation of 70 meters. Cerro Morrillo, a rocky knob 60 meters tall, marks the southwest end of the island. Visitors land at a large dock which leads to a visitor center with covered picnic tables and exhibits. The low, four-acre, flat-topped Cayo Morellito is about 200 meters to the west.

Viewing Information: The island has many species of lizards including 3 geckos, 2 Ameiva, 3 Anolis and iguanas. Omnivorous Ameivas 14 inches long and as thick as a broomstick scavenge for crumbs in the picnic area, as do pearly-eyed thrashers. On the shorelines, ruddy turnstones, American oystercatchers, and great blue herons are present year-round. Red-billed and white-tailed tropicbirds nest on Cerro Morrillo, except in the summer. Magnificent frigatebirds, brown boobies, and pelicans all nest on Cayo Morellito. The Puerto Rican racer is abundant and conspicuous. Agoutis, small rabbit-like mammals from Central America, have maintained a population since their introduction in the 1960s. A shallow reef off the northeast coast has a marked snorkel trail and allows viewing of many colorful reef fish including spotted eagle rays, trumpetfish, squirrelfish, morays, red hind, and many species of snappers, grunts, and parrotfish.

Directions: *The island is 8 miles southeast of the town of Ponce located on the south coast of Puerto Rico. Local operators provide ferry service to the island from Ponce.*

Ownership: Puerto Rico Department of Natural and Environmental Resources, P.O. Box 9066600, Puerta de Tierra, San Juan, PR 00906; (787) 724-2816

Size: Caja de Muertos—412 acres; Cayo Morellito—4 acres

Closest Town: Ponce

Tropicbirds nest on small islands in holes in steep cliffs or natural caves under piles of boulders.
DAVID W. NELLIS

Description: The reserve has a variety of habitats including subtropical dry forest, fringing and basin mangroves, salt flats, seagrass beds, and coral reefs.

Viewing Information: A population of about 300 manatees at the site is the second largest assemblage of this endangered marine mammal in Puerto Rico. Look for them near the boat ramp in Aguirre where the power plant discharges fresh water into Jobos Bay. The high water quality is demonstrated by the presence of mangrove oysters which grow attached to the stilt roots of red mangroves. Endangered yellow-shouldered blackbirds and Puerto Rican plain pigeons are found in the uplands while great blue herons, snowy egrets, and night herons feed in the shallow water and along the shoreline.

Directions: *From Ponce, take Highway 52 east to the Salinas exit for Hwy 1. Take Hwy 1 south to Hwy 3. Turn east on Hwy 3, then south on Hwy 705 to Aguirre. In Aguirre, the visitor center is at kilometer 2.3 on the main street. Several guides provide small boat trips into the reserve.*

Ownership: U.S. Government, National Estuarine Research Reserve System. (787) 853-4617 and Puerto Rico Department of Natural and Environmental Resources, P.O. Box 9066600, Puerta de Tierra, San Juan, PR 00906; (787) 721-5495

Size: 2,883 acres

Closest Towns: Ponce, to the west, and Guayama, to the east, have tourist facilities.

PUERTO RICO SOUTH COAST

Manatees are marine mammals reaching lengths of 15 feet and weighing up to 2000 pounds but usually weigh less than that. They move sedately through shallow water while grazing on pastures of marine grass. SUSAN SPECK

38. AGUIRRE STATE FOREST

Description: This dry forest is located on a coastal barrier dune peninsula with sandy beach on the south (ocean) side, gradually blending into mangroves on the north (lagoon) side. A parking area and boardwalk through the mangroves is being developed.

Viewing Information: Brown pelicans, ruddy turnstones, and black-necked stilts can be seen along the shorelines with gulls and terns joining them in the spring and summer. The chestnut manniken, intoduced from Asia, is common in the upland scrub. White-crowned pigeons nest in the tall stands of red mangrove. Manatees, herons, and egrets are best appreciated by meandering the serpentine creeks and mangrove cays by kayak, canoe, or small boat.

Directions: From San Juan, take Highway 52 south 34 miles to Hwy 53. Follow Hwy 53 east to Guayama and turn west on Hwy 3 for 4 miles to Hwy 7710, which leads southwest through the forest.

Ownership: Puerto Rico Department of Natural and Environmental Resources, P.O. Box 9066600, Puerta de Tierra, San Juan, PR 00906; (787) 721-5495

Size: 2,442 acres

Closest Town: Guayama is 5 miles to the northeast.

The little blue heron walks slowly or stands and waits in shallow water for the approach of the small fish which make up its diet.
JOSÉ COLÓN

ST. THOMAS, U.S. VIRGIN ISLANDS

(see map on pages 12–13)

39. BENNER BAY POND

Description: This small lagoon has a strip of mangrove forest at its mouth and many clumps of red, black, and white mangroves and buttonwood along the shoreline. The bay is very shallow and subject to tidal influence, so the shallows may be exposed or covered depending on the state of the tide.

Viewing Information: This bay is a haven for water birds. At low tide the exposed mud flats provide excellent feeding opportunities for shorebirds such as willets and black-necked stilts. As the tide rises, many small and juvenile fish move into the shallows of the bay and provide food for great blue herons, great egrets, snowy egrets, and little blue herons. Green herons and black-crowned and yellow-crowned night herons lurk in the mangroves catching unwary crabs and fish. Osprey soar overhead before diving and catching mullet in the shallows. Brown pelicans crash dive into schools of bait fish while gulls and terns pick single fish from near the surface. When the salinity is reduced by runoff from nearby uplands, several species of water weeds proliferate and attract large flocks of white-cheeked pintails.

Directions: *From Charlotte Amalie, take Highway 30 east about 3 miles to the T-intersection with Hwy 32. Turn right and drive about 1.5 miles on Hwy 32 until you see a road with a sign for Compass Point Marina. The road to the marina circles the bay and allows a scenic overview. Park at the marina and walk to the edge of the lagoon.*

Ownership: Virgin Islands Government

Size: 5 acres

Closest Towns: The village of Red Hook is 1.2 miles east; the metropolitan downtown district of Charlotte Amalie is 5 miles west.

The black-crowned night heron feeds primarily at night on crabs and fish captured between mangrove roots and in shallow water.

PETE CARMICHAEL

69

40. COW AND CALF ROCKS

Description: Cow and Calf Rocks are surface extensions of a rocky, coral-encrusted outcrop that rises out of surrounding waters about 70 feet deep. The shallow waters offer interesting snorkeling and the deeper parts dramatic structures for scuba diving.

Viewing Information: The rocks are encrusted with colorful species of fire, star, elkhorn, finger, and pillar corals in varying hues. Particularly striking is the abundant sponge community, which includes many vase, encrusting, rope, lumpy, and tubular sponges in vivid colors. On the southern side of the rocks are three open-ended caves in which scuba divers can observe schools of iridescent coppery glassy sweepers, large snappers, and lobsters. Crevices house myriad cryptic fishes and invertebrates such as blennies, green morays, small octopi, peppermint shrimp, and the translucent purple Peterson's cleaning shrimp.

Brown boobies, pelicans, and oystercatchers, regularly perch on these rocks while scanning nearby waters for schools of baitfish. In the summer, laughing gulls, terns, and brown noddies, are also present.

Directions: *This site is accessible only by boat. Rental boats and charts are available in the Red Hook area. All of the local dive shops provide dive trips to this site.*

Ownership: Virgin Islands Government

Size: The exposed rocks are only a few square yards in extent, but the reef and rocky outcrops cover about 10 acres.

Closest Towns: Charlotte Amalie. Many related facilities are available at Red Hook and Cruz Bay, St. John.

The sergeant major is found in tidepools along the shoreline, in midwater, and among the coral and sponges on reefs. STEVE SIMONSEN

41. CORAL WORLD AND COKI BEACH

Description: Descend 15 feet under the sea for a 360-degree view of a natural coral reef from Coral World's Underwater Observatory. Non-captive fish come and go freely. Indoor and outdoor exhibits, including a predator tank and mangrove lagoon, focus on Caribbean fauna and flora. Adjacent to Coral World is picturesque Coki Beach, which provides opportunity for snorkeling and scuba diving.

Viewing Information: Outside the windows at Coral World's underwater observatory see trumpetfish, grouper, squirrelfish, barracuda, and jack. From the top level, view frigatebirds, pelicans, and boobies. Outdoor pools feature sea turtles, stingrays, and juvenile sharks. The Marine Gardens present marine life—including seahorses, garden eels, cherubfish, moray eels, octopus, and live corals—in re-creations of their natural habitats. The 80,000-gallon Caribbean Reef Encounter surrounds visitors with live corals and hundreds of coral reef fishes. At Coki Beach, palometa and mojarra are found on the shallow, sandy bottom. Grunts, parrotfish, and queen triggerfish are commonly seen among the coral.

Directions: *From Charlotte Amalie, take Highway 38 (Smith Bay Road) east about 5 miles to the intersection of Hwy 388. Turn east. Coral World and Coki Beach are at the end of the road, about 0.5 mile.*

Ownership: Coki Beach—Virgin Islands Government; Coral World—privately owned

Size: Coki beach—2 acres; Coral World—4.5 acres

Closest Town: The only town on the island is Charlotte Amalie.

The reef tank at Coral World allows a diverse perspective while viewing a great variety of colorful and varied reef fish. CORAL WORLD

CARIBBEAN SEA TURTLES

by Ralf Boulon

Three species of marine turtles are found in the Virgin Islands: the hawksbill, the leatherback, and the green.

The hawksbill turtle relies on our coral reefs for food and ledges to rest under. Hawksbills nest on nearly all Virgin Islands' beaches in every month of the year, but the peak season is July through November. The largest aggregations of hawksbills are on Buck Island, Sandy Point, and the east end beaches of St. Croix. Most juvenile and adult hawksbills remain in the same area for life, though banded adults have been recaptured on other Caribbean islands.

HAWKSBILL

STEVE SIMONSEN

Young green turtles are commonly found in shallow bays feeding on sea grasses but are rarely found here as adults.

Leatherbacks nest primarily on Sandy Point, St. Croix, and in lesser numbers on several other St. Croix beaches. Sandy Point is of particular interest because it is the location of the largest known nesting aggregation of leatherbacks on U.S. territory. They can lay up to eleven nests in a season (March through July), averaging 80 yolked and 30 yolkless eggs per nest.

STEVE SIMONSEN

GREEN SEA TURTLE

Turtle populations in the Virgin Islands have diminished due to nest poaching, taking of adults, and habitat loss.

Turtles are protected by law and recovery teams have developed conservation strategies to prevent any further decline in local marine turtle stocks. With continued protection and management, our sea turtle populations should continue their recovery to the levels seen in the past.

LEATHERBACK

PETER DUTTON

42. MANGROVE LAGOON MARINE RESERVE AND WILDLIFE SANCTUARY

Description: This site is a complex series of small islands fringed with red mangroves and interspersed with shallow marine grass beds and a sandy bottom.

Viewing Information: The mangroves provide nesting and roosting sites for many birds. Most commonly seen are great blue herons, little blue herons, cattle egrets, green herons, tricolored herons, night herons, and snowy egrets. white-cheeked pintails are present all year and ospreys are present in the winter. Yellow warblers are abundant and feed on insects in the mangroves. On Cas Cay, nature trails with interpretive signs provide access to typical seashore and dry forest vegetation inhabited by land crabs, hermit crabs, several species of lizards, and numerous species of migratory songbirds. Tropicbirds may often be seen by looking south from the higher elevations of the island. Snappers, grunts, butterflyfish, wrasses, damsel fish, and barracuda are commonly seen when snorkeling in the warm, shallow water along the mangroves. Large snook and tarpon often rest by day in the shade of overhanging mangroves. Conch, upside-down jellyfish, hawksbill and green turtles, rays, and lobsters are found in nearby shallow grass beds while brown pelicans and boobies dive on shoals of silvery baitfish.

Directions: *From Charlotte Amalie, take Highway 30 to Hwy 32. Turn right, and after driving 0.5 mile, the refuge will be on your right. A private company provides guided kayak tours of the lagoon from this site. Another access point is available by taking Route 311 to the southern end and snorkeling in the channel between Patricia Cay and Long Point.*

Ownership: Virgin Islands Government

Size: 680 acres

Closest Town: Charlotte Amalie

The cryptically colored green heron fishes along the shoreline and often perches on roots and branches projecting out of the water.
GIFF BEATON

43. CAS CAY WILDLIFE SANCTUARY

Description: Cas Cay is a small, dry tropical island whose primary features are controlled by the wind and the sea. On the east, facing the tradewinds and prevailing waves, is a 99-foot-tall hill of hard, erosion-resistant, metamorphic rock. Coral rubble and sand have accumulated on the leeward side of the hill to make a well-vegetated flat area to the west. The west end of the cay has been overwashed by waves of recent hurricanes and has been subject to human alteration by harvest of sea bird eggs, whelks, and wood.

Viewing Information: The ridge trail ascends the eastern hill and provides a broad vista of the lagoon and nearby islands. Red-billed tropicbirds nest under boulders on the steep southern slope of the ridge in the winter. White-tailed tropicbirds are often present in the summer. The ridgetop plateau is heavily windswept, but has endemic orchids and other interesting plants growing in protected areas behind boulders or shrubs. The western flat part of the cay is dominated by *Tabebuia,* a deciduous tree with the English misnomer of white cedar or pink cedar, and gumbo-limbo trees with seashore plants such as sea grape, manchineel, haiti-haiti, and mangroves. The island has anole, ameiva, and gecko lizards, and many sea birds can be seen flying and feeding near the island.

Directions: *Take Highway 30 or 38 east to Hwy 32 and continue east to the Mangrove Lagoon. Several marinas in the area can provide transport to Cas Cay and an ecotourism company rents kayaks which can be used for the short paddle to Cas Cay. Land on the west end of the island in one of the gaps in the mangroves.*

Ownership: Virgin Islands Government. Cas Cay is part of the Cas Cay/Mangrove Lagoon Marine Reserve and Wildlife Sanctuary.

Size: 14 acres

Closest Towns: The village of Red Hook can provide most daily needs. The town of Charlotte Amalie is 5 miles west.

Terrestrial hermit crabs have a body shape that allows them to back into snail shells and carry them about for protection. They enter the sea only once per year for a breeding orgy in August.
DAVID W. NELLIS

44. SABA ISLAND WILDLIFE REFUGE

Description: Saba is a large, triangular island with three small peaks composed of highly metamorphosed igneous rocks. The highest point on the island is 200 feet above sea level. The west-facing shoreline is protected from prevailing swells and usually provides a protected anchorage and a sandy beach. The north-facing slopes are gentle, but become steep at higher elevations. The south side of the island has eroded into steep rugged cliffs with a surface of loose weathered rock. The island is vegetated by a tall introduced grass, sedges, cacti, and thickets of vines and shrubs.

Viewing Information: During spring and summer, Saba Island has the largest colony of sea birds in the Virgin Islands, composed primarily of 30,000 sooty terns with lesser numbers of brown noddies, bridled terns, roseate terns, and laughing gulls. Two salt ponds provide habitat for white-cheeked pintails, yellow-crowned night herons, and black-necked stilts, with yellow warblers in the fringing mangroves. Trails are marked for use in the summer breeding season and in the winter season when sea birds are not breeding. A trail leads from the sandy beach to a bird-watching blind on the shore of the east pond. Virgin Islands regulations require that all visitors to the island be accompanied by a licensed sea bird guide. A coral reef community with many colorful fish is just offshore of the northeast-facing cobble beach.

Directions: *The island is about 3 miles southwest of the airport and is accessible only by boat. You can approach the sandy beach from the west and anchor near shore.*

Ownership: Virgin Islands Government

Size: 30.2 acres   **Closest Town:** Charlotte Amalie

Thousands of sooty terns come to nest on small islands in Puerto Rico and the Virgin Islands in early May. They usually depart by September and are absent in the winter months. JOSÉ COLÓN

ST. THOMAS, U.S. VIRGIN ISLANDS

75

ST. JOHN, U.S. AND BRITISH VIRGIN ISLANDS *(see map on pages 12–13)*

45. DRUNK BAY AND SALTPOND BAY

Description: These two bays are on opposite sides of a peninsula which contains a salt pond. Drunk Bay faces into the wind and has considerable wave action with a beach which grades from sand on the north to boulders on the south. Saltpond Bay has protected white sandy beaches. In dry weather, the pond evaporates and local residents still follow the custom of gathering salt crystals from the pond bottom. Ram Head is a high, rugged, rocky peninsula extending south between the two bays.

Viewing Information: The thick, thorny scrub vegetation adjacent to the trails harbors such permanent residents as smooth-billed anis, bananaquits, and bullfinches. The 0.75-mile trail to mountainous Ram Head passes habitat dominated by cacti. The 200-foot cliffs at the end of the trail allow good views of tropicbirds soaring from their nests in rock crevices. Snorkelers in Drunk Bay can observe coral, sea fans, and many species of colorful reef fish. The rocky margins of Saltpond Bay and the enclosed grass beds allow snorkeling to view. Flounder, stingrays, and goatfish are above the sand while trunkfish and parrotfish are found on the grass beds.

Directions: *From Cruz Bay, take VI 10 about 6 miles east and turn right at the junction of VI 107. Drive about 3.9 miles to the parking area for the Saltpond Bay Trail. A trail leads down to the fluffy white sand beach. If you walk south to the end of the beach, you will encounter the trail south to Ram Head.*

Ownership: The peninsula is part of Virgin Islands National Park, Cruz Bay, St. John, VI 00830; (340) 776-6201

Size: The peninsula is about 125 acres.

Closest Towns: Cruz Bay, St. John

This salt pond evaporates in the dry season and allows a traditional harvest of salt crystals.
STEVE SIMONSEN

46. EAGLE SHOALS

Description: The shoal is a rise of coral-encrusted rock which reaches within 6 feet of the surface from surrounding waters 90 feet deep.

Viewing Information: This magnificent dive site can be observed snorkeling from the surface, but is better appreciated with scuba gear. The fish in the shallow waters are sergeant majors, several species of damsels, and schools of blue chromis. In 20 to 40 feet of water, one can see all the typical reef fish including schoolmaster and mangrove snappers, queen triggerfish, gray and French angels, red hind, black-tip sharks, and jacks. Under the many ledges and cracks are copper sweepers, jackknife fish, and squirrelfish. Hawksbill turtles often wedge themselves between rocks or in caves while they sleep. A cathedral-like arched cave with entrances from several sides has small holes in the roof which allow beams of sunlight to penetrate and illuminate the interior enough to observe the thousands of fish which congregate in the cave. Many colorful fairy basslets swim upside down against the roof of the cave and take shelter among the colonies of cave coral.

Directions: This site is accessible only by boat. The center of Eagle Shoals is 0.75 mile south of the west end of Leduck Island, off the east coast of St. John. For those without navigational equipment, if you line up the south tip of Ram Head with Buck Island and travel east on that heading until the east end of Leduck Island is under the notch in the skyline of St. John produced by Haulover Bay, you will be over the center of Eagle Shoals.

Ownership: Virgin Islands Government

Size: The most interesting parts are the 4 acres or so near the center of the shoal, but the coral-encrusted rise covers about 80 acres of seabed.

Closest Town: Coral Bay, St. John

Fairy basslets prefer to live in caves and under overhangs where they often swim upside down with their bellies next to the ceiling. STEVE SIMONSEN

47. FRANCIS BAY POND

Description: This pond was a deep bay which had a berm built across the mouth by wave action. The berm is now a consolidated dune with tropical dry forest vegetation thriving on it. Depending on runoff, the mangrove-enclosed pond is often considerably less salty or more salty than the sea. Fluctuating water levels expose or submerge foraging habitat for many water birds. The west side of the berm is the beautiful and relatively unused Francis Bay Beach.

Viewing Information: This pond is often a stopping point for migratory birds such as greater yellowlegs, spotted sandpipers, blue-winged teals, and ruddy turnstones in the spring and fall. Resident birds include herons, egrets, Caribbean coots, and American coots. White-cheeked pintails nest near the pond and raise their ducklings in the pond. The mangrove cuckoo is found in the thickets around the pond. Five species of pigeons and doves along with many wintering warblers can be seen in the adjacent uplands.

Directions: *Take Highway 20 (North Shore Road) north and east toward Annaberg. At the T-intersection turn left toward Maho Campground, then park near the old stone storehouse. Take the trail north from the east side of the building about 300 yards to an overlook with a bench. Continue on the trail to circle the pond. A small boardwalk into the pond is connected to the trail. If you drive past the storehouse and follow the dirt road to the right you will pass a low spot paved with cement which marks the 150-yard path to the 50-foot-long boardwalk. Parking and restrooms are available at the end of the road.*

Ownership: Virgin Islands National Park, Cruz Bay, St. John, VI 00830; (340) 776-6201

Size: 20 acres

Closest Town: Cruz Bay, St. John

The white-cheeked pintail is a year-round resident which often nests on offshore cays but raises its young on salt ponds.
BRUCE HALLETT

Description: The Norman Island sea caves are reputed to have been the source of pirate treasure recovered by local fishermen who sought refuge from a rainstorm in the caves. These caves are actually the result of wave erosion of a soft spot in the metamorphic rock of the island and only penetrate about 200 feet into the cliff.

Viewing Information: As you tie your boat to a mooring, the resident fish begin to assemble and will swarm around you in dense schools as you enter the water. Black-bar soldierfish and copper sweepers, which normally reside in dark holes in the reef by day, form schools in open water just inside the cave mouth. If you swim into the back of the cave, you will almost always see bats hanging from the ceiling. Three species may be present, the Jamaican fruit bat, the cave bat, and the fishing bat, which catches fish near the water surface.

Directions: The caves are about 5 miles southwest of Road Town or 3 miles southeast of East End, St. John, at 18° 19' N and 64° 38' E. If you are piloting your own boat, please tie to a mooring and avoid dropping an anchor which will damage the coral. Several private individuals and companies offer day trips to the caves from Cruz Bay, Caneel Bay, and Coral Bay, St. John; and Road Town, Tortola.

Ownership: British Virgin Islands, National Parks Trust

Size: 3 acres

Closest Towns: Road Town, Tortola, or Coral Bay, St. John

Blue tangs are common herbivorous fish which sometimes congregate in large schools. STEVE SIMONSEN

ST. JOHN, U.S. AND BRITISH VIRGIN ISLANDS

The petroglyphs at the base of the Reef Bay waterfall may have been made by pre-European natives or a colony of escaped slaves. STEVE SIMONSEN

Description: The 2.6-mile Reef Bay Trail can be accessed by land at the trailhead on Highway 10 or by boat at the Reef Bay Beach. Park rangers lead a popular trip three times a week which includes transportation to the trailhead and a boat ride from the lower end of the trail to Cruz Bay. The trail descends more than 900 feet between Centerline Road and the beach at Reef Bay. About three-quarters of the way down the trail from the road, a spur trail about 300 yards long leads to a small waterfall. Petroglyphs attributed to native Arawaks are carved on the north side of the smooth rock at the bottom of the falls.

Viewing Information: The pool at the bottom of the falls has freshwater shrimp and mountain mullet with white-lipped frogs giving their *pink-pink-pink* calls in the nearby vegetation. In the dry season, when this is the only water within several miles, many birds come here to drink. In the forest along the trail you will hear and perhaps see smooth-billed anis, bananaquits, fruit pigeons, zenaida doves, and bridled quail-doves. As you approach the lower end of the trail, the 3-inch-diameter burrows beside the trail are inhabited by large vegetarian land crabs. The reefs offer interesting snorkeling on calm days. About 200 feet from the beach is a well-preserved sugar factory ruin.

Directions: *From Cruz Bay, take Highway 10 east 3.8 miles to the marked trailhead. Take the trail south toward Reef Bay. The spur trail to the waterfall is the only trail to the west and is marked with a sign.*

Ownership: Virgin Islands National Park, Cruz Bay, St. John, VI 00830; (340) 776-6201

Size: The National Park takes up three-quarters of the land on St. John.

Closest Towns: Cruz Bay, the only town on St. John, is 3.8 miles to the west and the small community of Coral Bay is 2.8 miles to the east.

WILLIAM STELZER

ST. JOHN, U.S. AND BRITISH VIRGIN ISLANDS

Description: Waterlemon Cay is a small island of metamorphic rock in Leinster Bay. Most of the shoreline is rocky, with a sandy beach on the southeast of the island which extends as a shallow sandbar to the east. The island has remarkable biodiversity for its size with 78 species of plants. As you are walking along the shoreline from Annaberg, the adjacent bay is a favorite overnight anchorage for transient yachts.

Viewing Information: To the north of the trail from Annaberg are many patch reefs in 6 feet of very clear water. A bit farther out is a coral-encrusted ledge which drops to 20 feet and provides habitat for many reef fish such as sergeant major, blue chromis, parrotfish, and queen triggerfish. To the southeast of the trail, where the shoreline turns north, is a shallow pond frequented by black-necked stilts and other shorebirds. Waterlemon Cay is used as a roost by brown pelicans, brown boobies, and other sea birds. Yellow warblers, bananaquits, and doves nest and feed on the cay. The reefs around the cay have many species of coral, and sea fans, doctorfish, brown chromis, four-eyed butterfly fish, grunts, and squirrelfish. Hawksbill and green turtles can be seen surfacing in the central part of the bay, or you may see one sleeping on the bottom.

Directions: *From Cruz Bay take Highway 20 north and east about 5.3 miles, then follow the signs to the ruins of the Annaberg sugar mill. Park at the mill and walk east 0.8 mile on the shoreline trail around Waterlemon (Leinster) Bay. A short swim is required to reach the island from St. John.*

Ownership: Virgin Islands National Park, Cruz Bay, St. John, VI 00830; (340) 776-6201

Size: The Virgin Islands National Park on St. John occupies 9,485 acres of land and 5,650 acres of water. It encompasses about three-quarters of the land on St. John.

Closest Town: Cruz Bay is the only significant town on St. John.

Queen angelfish eat living sponges and other invertebrates from the reef. The juveniles are even more spectacularly colored than the adult shown here.
SUSAN SPECK

51. WRECK OF THE RHONE

Description: The Royal Mail Ship Rhone was launched in 1865 and was washed ashore on Salt Island by the hurricane of 1867. The storm broke the vessel into two parts and washed them into nearby deeper water. The ship was originally 310 feet long with a beam of 40 feet. The stern of the vessel, with the huge propeller intact, is now in 30 feet of water. The midsection and various parts are scattered down the slope to a depth of 80 feet. The mostly intact, 150-foot bow section lies on its right side in 70 to 80 feet of water.

Viewing Information: The Wreck of the Rhone and the waters that surround it are a British Virgin Islands National Park. All artifacts and marine life are completely protected. After 130 years under water, the wreck is heavily encrusted with marine growth. The abundant fishes include yellowtails, sergeant majors, jacks, grunts, queen, french and gray angelfish, squirrelfish, and snappers. A jewfish over 300 pounds is regularly seen lurking in the wreck. Many of the fish will eagerly approach a diver to be fed.

Directions: The Wreck of the Rhone is just to the west of Salt Islands' Black Rock Point. Many of the commercial dive operators on St. Thomas, St. John, and Tortola offer regularly scheduled trips to the Rhone. If you are traveling in your own boat, you may not anchor on the wreck. Mooring buoys for visitors are very close to the wreck, just west of Black Rock Point.

Ownership: British Virgins Islands, National Parks Trust

Size: 20 acres

Closest Towns: Road Town, Tortola, is 6 miles northwest, and Coral Bay, St. John, is 12.5 miles west-southwest.

The protected status and prolific coral growth allow a great diversity and abundance of fish on the Rhone. STEVE SIMONSEN

ST. JOHN, U.S. AND BRITISH VIRGIN ISLANDS

ST. CROIX, U.S. VIRGIN ISLANDS

(see map on pages 12–13)

52. BOILER BAY

Description: This clear, shallow bay is ideal for snorkeling, protected from large waves by an offshore fringing reef. The site is undeveloped with a dirt road giving access to the shoreline and informal parking under the trees or along the beach. The bay has small and large patch reefs which support many types of coral and algae.

Viewing Information: Snorkeling in a meandering path through the patch reefs, or boilers, you will see staghorn coral, elkhorn coral, brain coral, and star coral. The flexible soft corals include sea fans and sea whips. Numerous anemones twist their variously colored tentacles, while sea urchins wave their needle-like spines. Do not touch the mustard-colored fire coral, which is found encrusting some of the shallower rocks. Fire coral can inject a toxin which induces a burning sensation on the skin for up to an hour. Many species of reef fish including parrotfish, tang, blue chromis, and creole wrasse hover near the refuge provided by the patch reefs. The antennae of occasional lobsters can be seen protruding from their dens at the base of the coral. In small caves and holes in the coral, you will see copper sweepers, black-bar soldierfish, drums, and squirrelfish. On the sand between the patch reefs are goatfish rooting for invertebrates and lizardfish waiting for small fish to come within range of a sudden dash.

Directions: *Take Highway 82 (East End Road) east from Christiansted 9 miles. About 0.5 mile past Cramer Park a dirt road to the left provides access to Boiler Bay. A second dirt road about 0.25 mile farther provides access to the east end of the bay.*

Ownership: Virgin Islands Government

Size: 64 acres

Closest Town: Christiansted

Squirrel fish generally stay near cracks and crannies in coral by day but venture out to feed at night.
SUSAN SPECK

Description: Buck Island is a moderately steep island covered with tropical dry forest. The vegetation is lower and dryer on the east (windward) end of the island with larger trees and more open forest on the north and west. A small dock on the south side allows for stepping ashore on the island without getting your feet wet. One hiking trail traverses the island from the south to the northwest and provides access to an overlook and various habitat types. The southwest coast of the island has a beautiful sandy beach. A barrier reef protects the island on the north and east sides. Inside the lagoon formed by the reef is a marine garden made up of many smaller patch reefs and coral heads.

Viewing Information: Flowering frangipani and orchids are common along the trails. Large terrestrial hermit crabs living in seashells and the St. Croix anolis lizard are common along the trails. Brown pelicans nest and magnificent frigatebirds roost, displaying their bright red, balloon-like throat pouches. A small salt pond and the shoreline are often used by several species of herons and other shorebirds. A colony of least terns nests on the beach from May to July. The beach is used at night for nesting by sea turtles. Commercial tour boats moor near the underwater trail and provide guided snorkeling tours to see coral grottos, many species of colorful and exotic fish, sea fans, and living sponges.

Directions: *As you leave Christiansted harbor, the island is visible to the northeast. Access is only by boat. Many concessionaires provide transportation and guided snorkel tours from the waterfront in Christiansted to the island.*

Ownership: Virgin Islands National Park, Christiansted, St. Croix, VI; (809) 773-1460

Size: The monument is 880 acres, of which 180 acres is the island, and the balance is the surrounding shallow marine community.

Closest Town: Christiansted, St. Croix

Buck Island is noted for its great diversity of coral which can be observed while snorkeling along a marked underwater trail.
STEVE SIMONSEN

ST. CROIX, U.S. VIRGIN ISLANDS

Description: This site is the floor of a steep-walled valley which is one of the three watersheds in the Virgin Islands to have flowing fresh water year-round. A trickling stream and the highest rainfall found anywhere on the island keep the habitat very moist. Silk-cotton, mango, and hog plum trees make a high canopy which supports many bromeliads, orchids, and vines.

Viewing Information: There is no organized trail, but the walking is easiest if you follow the streambed. The pigeon family is very well represented with white-crowned and scaly-naped pigeons feeding and roosting in the tops of the trees while ground and zenaida doves look for seeds on open ground. Bridled quail-doves can often be heard before they are seen scratching and pecking in the leaf litter in the deep shade. Mangrove cuckoos are also heard more frequently than they are seen. Anoles and geckos are common. Mongooses may be seen by day and two species of large fruit bats are always present at dusk. Several types of freshwater shrimp along with the mountain mullet, or dagger, and several gobies, sedentary bottom-dwelling fish, may be found in the larger pools. The fish share the unusual life history of living as adults in freshwater with eggs and larvae developing in the sea.

Directions: From Frederiksted, take Highway 63 (the West Shore Road) north for 4 miles until it ends at the scenic drive (Hwy 78). Proceed on unpaved Hwy 78 until it turns left up the hill, then park and walk up the floor of the valley through the abandoned quarry to an unused vehicle path which follows the streambed.

Ownership: Virgin Islands Government

Size: 100 acres

Closest Town: Frederiksted

The white-crowned pigeon feeds on fruit and roosts in the tops of tall trees.
BRUCE HALLETT

Description: The edge of the geologic platform that supports St. Croix comes very close to shore at Cane Bay. It is possible to snorkel out from shore about 300 yards north, then descend with scuba gear to 70 feet and meet the wall which drops vertically over 1,000 feet.

Viewing Information: On the way out you will swim over a gradually descending bottom of sand and scattered corals until you come to the reef at about 50 feet. The reef is made up of many plate, lettuce, and star corals with increasing numbers of large sponges as you proceed over the edge and down the face. The reef is noted for having several old ships' anchors embedded in its coral. The many diverse and abundant species of fish include black durgon, sharks, blue chromis, creole wrasse, and queen triggerfish. Open ocean animals such as dolphins, whales, manta rays, and sea turtles can also be seen here. **CAUTION:** Keep track of your bottom time. This is a deep dive with lots of beautiful scenery to distract you.

Directions: *From Christiansted, take Highway 75 west 4 miles to Hwy 80. Follow Hwy 80 to the north, then west 5 miles to the boat ramp. Park at the boat ramp, enter the water, and swim north. Before descending, take a compass bearing on the boat ramp. Then when your dive is over, return along the bottom for a more gradual ascent.*

Ownership: Virgin Islands Government

Size: 50 acres

Closest Town: Christiansted

Blue chromis are often found in open water near coral reefs. STEVE SIMONSEN

ST. CROIX, U.S. VIRGIN ISLANDS

The vegetarian green iguana lives in trees and often seeks refuge by diving into the sea. PETE CARMICHAEL

Description: An old cart road travels up a steep-sided, forested valley past an abandoned dam which at one time provided the water supply to Frederiksted. The road is very narrow but has a few wide spots which allow you to park and walk along the road for viewing. A good place to park is the old quarry about 50 meters past the dam on the opposite side of the road. At the beginning of Creque Dam Road, a quaint hotel with a beachside restaurant offers horseback tours of the valley.

Viewing Information: This valley on the wet, western end of St. Croix has some of the most fully developed moist forest in the Virgin Islands. Huge silk-cotton, mango, and sandbox trees form a canopy which provides open shade for cocoa and coffee, which was cultivated in plantation days and continues to grow uncultivated. Scaly-naped pigeons call from the treetops while the booming call of the terrestrial bridled quail-dove is heard from the forest floor. The distinctive call of the mangrove cuckoo can often be heard before a rain shower passes. Locally, it's called the rain bird. With protection, iguanas are now repopulating the valley. If you drive the road after dark, you will see Jamaican fruit bats, cave bats, and the tiny, black, insect-eating roof bat in acrobatic flight.

Directions: *From Frederiksted, take Highway 63 north 1.5 miles to Hwy 58 (Creque Dam Road) and turn east. Viewing opportunities exist for the next 3 miles. For a pleasant return to Frederiksted, turn south on Hwy 765 (Annaly Road) and drive about 1 mile to the intersection of Hwy 76 (Mahogany Road). Turn west and continue until Hwy 76 intersects Hwy 63, 0.2 mile north of Frederiksted.*

Ownership: The land adjoining the road is in various public and private ownership.

Size: The watershed is about 1,000 acres.

Closest Town: Frederiksted

Cave bats prefer to roost in dark caves or in old masonry ruins. They venture forth at night to eat pollen and drink nectar from night blooming flowers.
DAVID W. NELLIS

ST. CROIX, U.S. VIRGIN ISLANDS

57. GREAT POND

Description: This site has a dirt wheel track to a small, very shallow lagoon which once was a salt pond but is now connected to the sea via a tidal creek. You can walk along the upland edges of the salt flats, but the mud gets quite sticky if you venture into the pond. The 10-inch tidal range in the Virgin Islands has considerable influence on covering and exposing the extensive mud flats. The berm to the south, which separates the lagoon from the sea, is vegetated with mangroves and salt-tolerant upland trees and shrubs. To the north are thickets of black, red, and white mangrove with water or mud flats in between. The mud flats grade into grassland on the west and acacia thorn-scrub to the east.

Viewing Information: Great egrets, snowy egrets, and little blue herons are almost always wading after fish in the shallows, while black-necked stilts, sandpipers, and plovers seek invertebrates in the exposed mud flats. Brown pelicans and royal terns dive after fish in the deeper water. In the winter and early spring, migrant ospreys fish over the pond. Bananaquits, grassquits, and gray kingbirds are common on the adjoining uplands. In May and June, least terns usually nest along the upper edges of the pond, while herons and egrets nest in the taller trees.

Directions: *From Christiansted, take Highway 82 east 3.1 miles. Turn right at the T-intersection with Hwy 60. Proceed south on Hwy 60 for 1.8 miles until you see an unimproved dirt road on the right leading 100 yards to the pond.*

Ownership: Virgin Islands Government

Size: 500 acres

Closest Town: Christiansted

The Yellow-crowned night heron is primarily active after sundown but may be seen foraging on fish and crabs along mangrove shorelines by day.
GIFF BEATON

Description: The refuge occupies a low limestone ridge, covered with sand, which projects to the southwest from St. Croix. The peninsula is covered with a community of tropical salt- and drought-tolerant plants such as sea grape and bay cedar. The Sandy Point orchid is quite common on shrubs and trees inland. The peninsula is rimmed with sandy beaches which are used by leatherback, green, and hawksbill turtles for nesting. The beach on the west is broad and clean, with clear water suitable for swimming and snorkeling. The refuge is open on Saturday and Sunday only.

Viewing Information: There are no marked trails, but you pass a large salt pond on your right 0.5 mile after you drive into the refuge. The pond usually has many waders such as great egrets, snowy egrets, and little blue herons, along with black-necked stilts, sandpipers, and plovers, as well as Bahama pintails. Least terns often nest on the widest part of the southwest beach and around the salt pond from May through August. Inland, yellow warblers are abundant and, with careful observation in the thick brush along the road, you may see one of the abundant but secretive small Indian mongooses. The refuge is closed to the public at night, but with prior reservations, small groups are allowed to accompany the team studying nesting sea turtles.

Directions: *Take any of the routes west from Christiansted until they intersect Highway 66 (Melvin H. Evans Highway). Follow it west to its end. Continue in the same direction 0.3 mile on a dirt road to the refuge entrance. After entering through the gate, continue for 1.2 miles to the end of the road and park.*

Ownership: U.S. Fish and Wildlife Service, Room 167, Federal Building 3013, Estate Golden Rock, Christiansted, St. Croix, VI 00820-435; (809) 773-4554

Size: 325 acres

Closest Town: Frederiksted

Leatherback turtles are the world's largest reptiles and live far from land in the open sea except when they return to their natal beach every other year to lay their eggs. Hatchlings leave the beach and do not return until many years later as adults to deposit eggs.
PETER DUTTON

ST. CROIX, U.S. VIRGIN ISLANDS

MONGOOSES

by David W. Nellis

Mongooses were introduced to the new world in 1872 when nine animals from Calcutta were released on a sugar cane plantation in Jamaica to control rats which destroyed much cane. The mongooses survived and reduced the rat populations while increasing their own populations. Planters from other islands heard of the great success and imported mongooses from Jamaica to most of the cane-growing islands. Although mongooses are diurnal and rats are nocturnal, mongooses have no trouble finding sleeping rats in cane fields. In forested areas the only rats that survive sleep in trees. Today mongooses reach an abundance of two per acre and eat insects such as grasshoppers, fruit, lizards, small birds, rats, mice, and crabs. They are fierce predators and have been known to kill deer fawns. Ground-nesting birds and snakes are particularly vulnerable to mongooses and several extinctions have been blamed on mongoose predation. Mongooses are a grizzled gray-brown, which enables them to hide in the grassy shrubland which they prefer. They feel very uneasy when exposed to hawks and thus are almost always running when you see one crossing the road. They acclimate readily to humans and often seek food scraps at picnic sites. This mongoose is the same species that Rudyard Kipling immortalized as Riki-tiki-tavi in *The Jungle Book*.

Mongooses are diurnal predators which eat fruits and vegetables but prefer to catch almost any animal small enough to overpower including crabs, insects, mice, and birds. DAVID W. NELLIS

59. UNIVERSITY OF THE VIRGIN ISLANDS WETLANDS RESERVE

Description: This wetland is a series of three coastal ponds which vary in salinity from brackish to three times as salty as seawater, depending on rainfall, evaporation, terrestrial runoff, and storms. The water level and salinity greatly influence the number of birds using the pond.

Viewing Information: Brown pelicans, least terns, and ospreys hover over the pond and dive for fish. White-cheeked pintails and common moorhens swim around the edges, while black-necked stilts and willets forage along the edges of the pond and nest on the sand and gravel berm in the spring. Large populations of tilapia and mosquito fish provide food for great egrets, snowy egrets, great blue herons, and night herons, all of which nest in the mangroves. At night, fishing bats scoop small fish from the pond. Terrestrial fiddler crabs, land crabs, and ghost crabs are numerous on the edges of the pond and the adjoining beach. On the surrounding uplands, kingbirds, bananaquits, mongooses, and anolis lizards are common. White-tailed tropicbirds nest on the cliffs to the east and can often be seen in their dramatic display flights over the water just south of the beach.

Directions: *From Frederiksted, travel east on Highway 66 to Hwy 81, turn south and cross Hwy 68, then proceed south 0.9 mile on a dirt road to the ponds. From Christiansted, travel west on Hwys 70 and 68 until you reach the junction of Hwy 81. Then turn left and follow directions above.*

Ownership: University of the Virgin Islands

Size: The three ponds total about 9 acres.

Closest Towns: Christiansted to the east and Frederiksted to the west.

The black-necked stilt is usually found probing for invertebrate prey in mud under shallow water. JOSÉ COLÓN

ST. CROIX, U.S. VIRGIN ISLANDS

INDEX

ABOUT THE AUTHOR

David W. Nellis earned his doctorate in wildlife biology from the University of Georgia. He has lived in the Virgin Islands, worked there as a wildlife biologist, and has been a frequent diver there for three decades. He has conducted research on mongooses, bats, sea birds, and feral burros. His work has required him to visit many small, uninhabited Caribbean islands, and he claims to be the only living person to have walked on all 52 of the U.S. Virgin Islands.

Discover the Thrill of Watching Wildlife.

 The Watchable Wildlife® Series

Published in cooperation with Defenders of Wildlife, these high-quality, full color guidebooks feature detailed descriptions, side trips, viewing tips, and easy-to-follow maps. Wildlife viewing guides for the following states are now available with more on the way.

Alaska
Arizona
California
Colorado
Florida
Indiana
Iowa
Kentucky
Massachusetts
Montana

Nebraska
Nevada
New Hampshire
New Jersey
New Mexico
New York
North Carolina
North Dakota
Ohio
Oregon

Puerto Rico &
  Virgin Islands
Tennessee
Texas
Utah
Vermont
Virginia
Washington
West Virginia
Wisconsin

Watch for this sign along roadways. It's the official sign indicating wildlife viewing areas included in the Watchable Wildlife® Series.

FALCON®